The Conscience of God

Andrea L. Russell

All scripture quotations are taken from the Young's Literal Translation of the Bible, translated by Robert Young.

Cover design by Andrea L. Russell

About the cover:
Several years ago, I saw this image of a face on the floor, and sketched it from memory. To me it appeared to be the marred face of Christ. Using the drawing to represent our loving Christ, I combined graphic elements to create the sky in the background. The severed and striped hands were introduced to show the suffering believers have experienced and continue to endure for our faith in Jesus Christ (I Peter 1:21).

Let us be diligent, spotless and unblameable (II Peter 3:14), as we wait on the Lord to make a new earth and new heavens, in which His righteousness dwells (II Peter 3:13). Also, may we obey God's commandments to love Him and to love others as ourselves (Luke 10:27).

The Conscience of God © 2014
www.theconscienceofgod.com

ISBN 978-0-578-18005-2

All rights reserved. No part of this publication may be reproduced, stored in a retrieval system or transmitted in any form by any means – electronic, mechanical, digital, photocopying, recording or any other – except for brief quotations in printed reviews, without the prior permission of the publisher. This is the complete and revised copy.

Printed in the United States of America

Dedication:

I dedicate this book to my loving and devoted parents,
Osra E. Russell and Irving A. Russell, Sr.

Special Thanks: I would like to thank: the Lord for answering my prayers and giving me the strength to complete the task of writing this book; my Mom for teaching and reminding me to pray and my Dad for overseeing it, as our family's provider; my sister Charmaine for her love, taking care of me after my mastectomy, lovingly providing clothing, being a listening ear and showing her love to my children; Caesar and Modupe, my brothers, for their love, devotion and concern, especially, during my chemotherapy treatments; Candace, my daughter, for watching over me and being my advocate; Patrick and Allyse, my son and daughter-in-law, for their kindness, generosity and love; Aunt Lydia Brown for reaching out to me and keeping tabs on my health; all my family, friends, neighbors; my faithful clients for staying with me through my illnesses; my pastor and his wife from my youth: Mrs. Anna Hairston and Reverend Dr. Otis Hairston, Sr. for teaching God's Word and being holy examples; Dr. Keith A. Troy for obediently guiding the churchgoers to walk in their gifts, and his wife, Mrs. Brenda Troy, for her selfless devotion to the community; Barb Lindsay for taking care of the children and walking them home after school; Pastor Josh Lively for his countless help and encouragement; Mrs. Sue Lively for working with my daughter, Candace, and the youth; Pastor Butler B'ynote' for helping me through tribulations and his wife, Tanya, for speaking words of wisdom to me; John and Jen Lindsay for considerable care; Tammy Titus for her gifts of love; Karl Road Day Women Bible Study Fellowship for eight great years; TJCII prayer group and Dawn Uhrick, for her time to thoughtfully read the first draft of this book; Millie Milam for setting the price, patiently waiting through revisions and for her feedback; Jana G. Cavalier for meticulously editing portions of the first draft; The Law Offices of Athena Inembolitis for patiently assisting me to keep my house and managing my affairs; my doctors for helping me to beat cancer; Connie Berry for being there after surgery; Victoria Cavendish for lovingly and selflessly helping with the garage ministry; Barb Long for volunteering her time to help the ministry; Darrah Courter for helping me in a time of crisis; Phyllis Tylor for providing assistance to me in my time of need; Citi Financial and other creditors for showing tremendous kindness, mercy and understanding to release my debts, to whom I am forever grateful; silent observers for praying; a stranger's encouraging look at the bank; construction companies and workers for helping my business; dear Shirley Cotter for editing. God richly bless all of you.

Preface

God is listening to the quiet whispers of the heart. We may often forget these unspoken glimpses of what we ponder or questions fleeting through our minds. For our benefit and others, God hears us and presents the answers in His time. God's pattern of thoughtful response reminds me of my father's gentle and calm demeanor. As a soft-spoken man, my father would listen and give wise counsel. Consistently thinking about others, my mother always would somehow know our need. The image of class, elegance, beauty and often commandingly fiery, mom would insist on speaking only once. Her poise with my father's calm demeanor and their combined dignity, intellect and wit are still with me forming an unbreakable bond. As I mature in Christ, I continue to discover valuable attributes of my parents' love. How God uses the memories of my mother and my father to enrich my life.

By experiencing the death of my parents, later in life, I know the value and uniqueness of a mother and a father. Without question, losing parents, at any age, is devastating and difficult to overcome. However, as I value my parents' treasures of love and devotion to our family, I pray that their passing will always be with me. God keep the wound of this loss fresh in my memory, to strengthen me as a mother to my two children and to console others who grieve.

Holding the position of Father to my children, Patrick and Candace, the Lord is my Father, as well as, my Husband and Healer. Truly, I am eternally grateful for the comfort, leadership and healing that God gives me. As a result, I am able to make key decisions for holy living and have completeness.

Purpose

Having a relationship with God, for me, is like water and sugar. He sweetens and melts me. A catalyst for change, the God of my salvation is actively adding His flavor to complete His good works in me. Staking a claim to the wonderful works of God would be foolish (Acts 12:23). Apostle Paul's message tells us to embrace the humble concept of service to God (Romans 12:1). In other words, it is not too much for God to ask us to be holy. Giving our bodies, souls and spirits completely to God makes the task easy and lightens the burden. It is pleasurable to serve God wholeheartedly without reservation. Thus my question to God: How does one have a heart after God like David? I now know it is really the other way around. One may certainly have a heart for God, but this search is for believers to know how to have God's heart.

Beginning as a whisper of my heart, after three years of reading the Old Testament, God gave me five characteristics. Those notes turned into the beginning of this book. Next, while participating in a Bible Study for eight years, I continued to write. The following five years, I studied the New Testament and spent several years writing, accompanied by prayer and fasting. Returning to the Old Testament, my journey took approximately sixteen years.

The scriptures show that God possesses these same characteristics and seeks David with His heart. Particular examples and details from David's life are present in this book, and significant experiences of God's divine hand come from others in the Bible, my loved ones and personal experiences.

The effort put forth here is to initiate, strengthen, and/or preserve a relationship between the Lord and the reader. Whether you are a believer in Jesus Christ or not, I pray that you read this book in its entirety. Let it inspire you to ask questions and to walk with the Lord wholeheartedly.

Like David, seek the Lord to prepare a clean heart, and renew a right spirit within you (Psalms 51:10). Desire for God to have a heart after you (I Samuel 13:14; Acts 13:22).

CONTENTS

Introduction	8
Scripture	10
Zeal	11
Boldness	17
Contentment	22
Humility	28
Faith	43
-Broma	47

Application & Information for Practical Use

Campaigns	63
Defeating the Enemies	65
Killing the Goliath in Us	75
Baptism by Fire	80
Tithing and Offering	83
The Conscience	84
Misunderstood Scriptures	101
Women	110
Prayer	114
Teaching	116
Temptation	124
God's Mercy	131
Love	136
Rapture Myth	140
My Testimony	146
About the Author	150

Notes & Diagrams

Introduction

God wants us to possess: zeal to have a jealous nature to serve Him; boldness for us to speak freely with confidence before God (I John 4:17), to confront the enemy, to ask questions, to speak the truth, to go where the Lord leads; contentment to serve and to praise God no matter the circumstances; humility, giving the believer a way to seek and to accept His guidance and direction; faith from God to have a confidence for the things hoped and a conviction for evidence of the unseen.

In High School, my Bible teacher, Mr. Woodring, said his Bible professor taught him that faith was overwhelming confidence. Those words echoed those of Apostle Paul who wrote, "And faith is of things hoped for a confidence, of matters not seen a conviction" (Hebrews 11:1).

King David possessed all of these qualities and therefore his devotion was the impetus for this inquiry. Despite his shortcomings, he was a man God sought according to His heart. David whom God, "… raised up over them one shepherd, And he hath fed them—my servant David, He doth feed them, and he is their shepherd, And I, Jehovah I am their God, And My servant David prince in their midst, I, Jehovah, have spoken" (Ezekiel 34:23-24).

How had David been a man after God's heart? After all, David summoned Bathsheba, committed adultery and impregnated her. In an attempt to hide the true identity of the baby's father, David called Bathsheba's husband, Uriah, from the battlefield to unite him with his wife. When this failed, David sent orders back with Uriah to his commander, Joab (II Samuel 11:14-15). By David's orders, Uriah was sent to fight on the front lines. In the heat of the battle, the other soldiers had been instructed to abandon Uriah to be killed.

Even though Uriah was one of David's thirty-seven valiant soldiers (II Samuel 23:39), he orchestrated Uriah's death. After Israel angered God, an adversary was near who tempted David to order Joab to number the

INTRODUCTION cont.

soldiers (II Samuel 24:2, I Chronicles 21:2). Joab protested the order of the king, but as expected David prevailed.

Thankfully, God looked at his heart and not on the outside as man (I Samuel 16:7). While he still honored God, David's proclivity for dealing with his faults was legendary. This has been a great lesson to all. Raising David to become king, God called him a man after His heart, and established that he was to do all His will (Acts 13:22). After David served God in his divine appointment, we saw he completed his specific tasks for God. Although, in many regards, he fell prey to sin, he repented. Throughout the scriptures, David truly loved the Lord and continued to serve God to do His will.

The scripture, Matthew 18:35, makes it very clear that we must forgive our brothers (believers). We forgive others as well, but this verse is speaking specifically to followers of Christ. Christ's blood provides the way for the Father to see us without condemnation. As believers, we know Jesus Christ is alive from the dead and call upon Him as our God and thank Him for our forgiveness (John 12:14-18, 36; Romans 10:9).

1 Peter 1:3-5

"Blessed [is] the God and Father of our Lord Jesus Christ, who according to the abundance of His kindness did beget us again to a living hope, through the rising again of Jesus Christ out of the dead, to an inheritance incorruptible, and undefiled, and unfading, reserved in heavens for you, who, in the power of God are being guarded, through faith, unto salvation, ready to be revealed in the last time."

Zeal

When David confronted Goliath, he emphasized the power of God and demonstrated his zeal to serve the Lord (I Samuel 17:45, 47). Through his worship and psalms, David's jealous nature for God was reflected in his behavior and writings. So much, that he sentenced Michal, his wife, to be childless after she dishonored him, because he danced before the Lord (II Samuel 6:20-23).

Certainly David's zeal honored the Lord; however, God originally possessed this attribute: "To the increase of the princely power, And of peace, there is no end, On the throne of David, and on his kingdom, to establish it, and to support it, In judgment and in righteousness, Henceforth, even unto the age, The zeal of Jehovah of Hosts doth this" (Isaiah 9:7).

Further, God clothed Himself with armor and zeal. " And He putteth on righteousness – as a breastplate, And an helmet of salvation on His head, And He putteth on garments of vengeance [for] clothing, And is covered, as [with] an upper-robe, [with] zeal" (Isaiah 59:17). Angered by commerce taking place in the temple, Jesus overturned the tables and said, " 'The zeal of Thy house did eat me up' " (John 2:17). See

Psalm 69:9, for further exploration, as well.

Just as God dressed Himself to defeat His enemies, God groomed David in the wilderness (I Samuel 17:37). In I Samuel 17:31, the words of David reached king Saul. David gave glory to God and exhibited several characteristics at once. Possessing boldness, he acknowledged God as he recounted his victory over a lion and a bear. To David this uncircumcised Philistine was none other (I Samuel 17:36). David experienced God's salvation and knew the Lord's people would prevail against Goliath, because he threatened what belonged to God, Israel. With fervor David said, " '… he [Goliath] hath reproached the ranks of the living God' " (I Samuel 17:26, 36).

Where is the fight in the Church? Currently, the same crises persist: Should women preach, just teach or just sit on the other side and be quiet? Should we sprinkle or immerse? Should we water baptize at all? Will Christians be 'raptured'? What color was Jesus? Do angels sing? Is there a God? Will people of other faiths go to Heaven or just Christians? Why did God allow sin? Is tomorrow promised? Are we sealed and always saved, even if we continue to sin?

Let us allow God to rule and to reign in our lives and take His advice: "but seek ye first the reign of God and His righteousness, and all these shall be added to you" (Matthew 6:33). One's speech and actions reveal the presence of righteousness (Luke 6:45; James 1:19-20). When God knocks, give Him a place to inhabit, to dwell. Then, His righteousness will be added to you and all of the things that God has for you. The Kingdom of God equates to the dominion of God. God's Kingdom is at hand and ready for all who seek after Him and desire to wear righteous garments, to flourish and grow with the seed firmly planted.

Many have fallen into traps laid by Satan to distract and to distort a simple message preached by Jesus and His servants: the Good News. Jesus, the Son of God, remained in those who believed (1 John 4:15-16). He finished all need for sacrifices for the forgiveness of sin. One road, Jesus Christ, past, present and future, has been the only way to eternal peace in Heaven. With Christ's help, believers have avoided pitfalls to practice pure religion. In fact, James defined, "religion pure and undefiled with the God and Father is this, to look after orphans and widows in their tribulation – unspotted to keep himself from the world" (James 1:27).

Christ prepares His brethren to be without spot or wrinkle as His bride for the marriage of the Lamb. Living holy, forsaking the flesh* combined with making choices for eternal blessing and not eternal damnation, is pure religion. A world without religion, as John Lennon's song "Imagine" describes, though it has some positive sentiments, points away from God to the "imagination of man that exalts itself above the knowledge of God" (II Corinthians 10:5).

*Flesh – Galatians 5:19-26:
"v. 19 And manifest also are the works of the flesh, which are: Adultery, whoredom, uncleanness, lasciviousness, v. 20 idolatry, witchcraft, hatred, strifes, emulations, wraths, rivalries, dissensions, sects, v.21 envyings, murders, drunkennesses, revellings, and such like, of which I tell you before, as I also said before, that those doing such things the reign of God shall not inherit. v. 22 And the fruit of the Spirit is: Love, joy, peace, long-suffering, kindness, goodness, faith, v.23 meekness, temperance: against such there is no law; v. 24 and those who are Christ's, the flesh did crucify with the affections, and the desires; v. 25 if we may live in the Spirit, in the Spirit also we may walk; v. 26 let us not become vain-glorious — one another provoking, one another envying!"

David and others in the Bible displayed great zeal in their service to God. John, in Revelation, wrote about being neither hot nor cold, but hot or cold. Not lukewarm and spewed out of God's mouth as the messenger informed the Laodiceans:

"… These things saith the Amen, the witness – the faithful and true – the chief of the creation of God; I have known thy works, that neither cold art thou nor hot; I would thou wert cold or hot. So – because thou art lukewarm, and neither cold nor hot, I am about to vomit thee out of my mouth; because thou sayest – I am rich, and have grown rich, and have need of nothing, and hast not known that thou art the wretched, and miserable, and poor, and blind, and naked, I counsel thee to buy from me gold fired by fire, that thou mayest be rich, and white garments that thou mayest be arrayed, and the shame of thy nakedness may not be manifest, and with eye-salve anoint thine eyes, that thou mayest see. 'As many as I love, I do convict and chasten; zealous then, and reform…" (Revelation 3:14-22).

Relying on earthly riches and thinking that that's all one needs is an illusion. God says the person is: " wretched, miserable, and poor, and blind, and naked." Why? Well, as one may guess, riches come and go, but Christ is eternal. Even if riches stay, that is not enough to satisfy the soul and the spirit. Neither will money buy a ticket to Heaven. Without the riches God offers, we are poor. Having monetary riches is not the problem, relying on them instead of God is. Also, how does someone, " 'buy gold fired by fire, that thou mayest be rich, and white garments' " to dress? The answer is with zeal, faith, boldness, humility to serve the Lord and contentment to obey His commands. When we hold fast to obey God and maintain our commitment to Him, we buy gold fired by fire. This sacrificial payment shows zeal within the believer and underscores a believer's service to God. Our white garments signify righteousness, to be worn after death, as a sign of our commitment to God while living on the earth.

Daniel's zeal allowed him to go without the King's portion of food. His commitment to the Lord caused him to rely on God to strengthen Shadrach, Meshach, Abednego and himself. This was a testament to his good purchase of Godly gold and white garments (Daniel 1:8-13). Also, by following God, their obedience gave them a holy expectancy. This expectation was fueled and set alight by zeal. Refusing to bow down to the golden image at the sound of the instruments and music (Daniel 3:5), Shadrach, Meshach and Abednego honored God. Their zeal caused them to defy the command of King Nebuchadnezzar. They said, "Lo, it is; our God whom we are serving, is able to deliver us from a burning fiery furnace; and from thy hand, O king, He doth deliver" (Daniel 3:17).

By forsaking King Nebuchadnezzar's idolatrous command, these men revered the Almighty God. Consequently, such acts became purchases from God of "gold fired by fire" these men were to be rich and to wear white garments. To show God's zeal for His children, His authority and His righteousness, He blocked the fire from harming the men and the smoke from leaving a scent on them (Daniel 3:27). In response to the men's zeal, God exerted His protection over them, canceled the sentence of King Nebuchadnezzar, and ultimately showed everyone present true power. Immediately, Nebuchadnezzar recognized the authority of God and made a decree allowing the men to serve the Lord, exclusively.

In actuality, Nebuchadnezzar had subjugated the people to worship an image representative of his limited authority. Although God specifically prohibited idol worship, fabrication and service, King Nebuchadnezzar was unwavering in his decision to execute anyone who refused to bow down to his god. Due to the hard stance taken by the king, several factors were in play. First, Nebuchadnezzar suffered from the root of deception or unbelief (Hebrews 3:12-13). Nebuchadnezzar only believed, when he saw the power of God. Second, the king was convinced that he was responsible for the success of his kingdom (Daniel 4:30). Third, the king gave glory to himself and not to God.

Turning to the New Testament, Paul writes, "and [it is] good to be zealously regarded, in what is good, at all times, and not only in my being present with you" (Galatians 4:18). Godliness and a jealous nature for God is exactly what Satan hates. That is why so many hurl false accusations at the Bible and the seed of Abraham. By warring against the righteous words and works of God, Satan unsuccessfully attempts to undermine the resolve of God's children. Take heart, "No weapon formed against thee prospereth, And every tongue rising against thee, In judgment thou condemnest. This [is] the inheritance of the servants of Jehovah, And their righteousness is of me, an affirmation of Jehovah!" (Isaiah 54:17).

The scripture Psalm 105:6, refers to the servant of Jehovah, the seed of Abraham: " O seed of Abraham, His servant, O sons of Jacob, His chosen ones." Also, as the seed of Abraham, now all believers are heirs together with Israel. This makes us a family of Jews and non-Jews. The blessings of Abraham fall to all of his offspring. Non-Jews are the spiritual offspring of Abraham, because of their love for the Jewish God (Galatians 3:29).

In no way does this cancel out the Jewish people and make Christians the substitution for Jews. One must be careful to avoid making the mistake spoken of in Revelation 3:9, "lo, I make of the synagogue of the Adversary those saying themselves to be Jews, and are not, but do lie; lo, I will make them that they may come and bow before thy feet, and may know that I loved thee." To prove a point, God will let the imposters bow at the feet of the Jewish believers. He will show them the consequences for trying to replace the Jews.

As the family of God, believers must strongly denounce false teachings and strive to unify God's body. We should elevate our fellow brothers and sisters, working to be one mentally and spiritually in Christ (Philippians 2:1-4).

Those who deceive and those who are deceived will experience an eternity in Hell. The Apostle John writes in Revelation 21:7-8, "…he who is overcoming shall inherit all things, and I will be to him – a God, and he shall be to me – the son, and to fearful, and unstedfast, and abominable, and murderers, and whoremongers, and sorcerers, and idolaters, and all the liars, their part [is] in the lake that is burning with fire and brimstone, which is a second death' " (Revelation 21:7-8). Rather than receiving curses, let us give honor to God and heap blessings on our heads. "Honour Jehovah from thy substance, And from the beginning of all thine increase; And filled are thy barns [with] plenty, And [with] new wine thy presses break forth" (Proverbs 3:9-10).

Boldness

"and Christ, as a Son over his house, whose house are we, if the boldness and the rejoicing of the hope unto the end we hold fast" (Hebrews 3:6).

"Having, therefore brethren, boldness for the entrance into the holy places, in the blood of Jesus" (Hebrews 10:19).

While David had boldness to confront Goliath, the enemy of Israel, Jesus described a different type of boldness, one of shameless persistence used to petition God. He told a story about a man who was unashamed to ask his neighbor for bread, in the night. To go to his neighbor, after he and his family had gone to bed was compared to how we must requisition God; persist with faith and without embarrassment (Luke11:5-10; http://biblehub.com/greek/335.htm).

At times, it is difficult to separate boldness from contentment, faith, zeal and humility, because they intertwine, existing simultaneously. In the book of Hebrews an example illustrating this point is found. Paul's boldness and humility allow him to instruct the Hebrews to live in brotherly love and to be hospitable. Also, he tells them to remember those imprisoned and mistreated. Paul continues to exhibit his zeal by emphasizing the importance of holy living, showing his contentment and faith to say without fear that the Lord is a helper.

"Let brotherly love remain; of the hospitality be not forgetful, for through this unawares certain did entertain messengers; be mindful of those in bonds, as having been bound with them, of those maltreated, as also yourselves being in the body; honorable [is] the marriage in all, and the bed undefiled, and whoremongers and adulterers God shall judge. Without covetousness the behaviour, being content with the things present, for He hath said, 'No, I will not leave, no, nor forsake thee,' so that we do boldly say, 'The Lord [is] to me a helper and I will not fear what man shall do to me' " (Hebrews 13:1-6).

God says honorable the marriage in all. The bed undefiled, whoremongers and adulterers, "God shall judge". That does not mean any act between married couples is undefiled. It simply means that marriage is honorable and God will judge those married in the bed as undefiled. Also, God judges whoremongers and adulterers. For example, Proverbs 6:29 says, "So [is] he who hath gone in unto the wife of his neighbour, None who doth touch her is innocent." In the current climate of sexual immorality, one must have boldness to stand for marriage and sexual morality. The choice one makes now determines ones eternity. How regrettable to hide behind the shelter of silence, than to speak out against fornication. Sex, outside of the marriage of two people, born of the opposite sex, is sin.

Once, I asked God how to lovingly speak to someone who had been hurt and had turned to an immoral, sexual relationship. I wondered how to address fornication, in particular homosexuality. God answered audibly, "It is better to comfort with the truth, than to pacify with a lie". I was chilled and realized that the Word had confirmed the Word, just as Jesus spoke in the temple. He said, " 'If ye remain in my word, truly my disciples ye are, and ye shall know the truth and the truth shall make you free' " (John 8:31-32).

Sin separates us from God and leads to death, "because he who is sowing to his own flesh, of the flesh shall reap corruption; and he who is sowing to the Spirit, of the Sprit shall reap life age-during" (Galatians 6:8; also, see Romans 8:4-6). Jesus asserts in the book of John that those who commit sin are servants to sin and do not remain in the house as a son (John 8:34 and 35). He maintains, " 'I am the way, the truth and the life no one doth come unto the Father, if not through me' " (John 14:6). Therefore, only Jesus makes a safe passage to truth and life, in order to come before the Father.

Every person has a moral obligation to be thankful to God. Let us not be thankless, refusing to give God glory, by changing His word to falsehoods and reducing our image of God to corruptible man and various animals (Romans 1). Rather, let us exalt God thanking Him for the open gate to the righteous (Psalm 118).

Today, there is a prevalent teaching that Jesus is not God, and that God is in every thing and creature. This teaching posits the existence of a collective consciousness. Once, while in a reading group, I remember encountering this ideology. Here is the facilitator's example: If the ocean represents God and you dip a cup into the body of water, you would be the content filling the cup. Of course, these teachings of idolatry are antithetical to worshipping Jesus, the Father and the Holy Spirit as one sovereign Lord or God. Believers in Christ worship the Creator and not the creation. God's law forbids making, serving or worshipping other gods (Exodus 20:1-5). Jesus creates all things (John 1:10), and manifests in unity with the Father and the Holy Spirit, individually and/or together. Creation is evidence of God and not to be the object of worship: "for the invisible things of Him from the creation of the world, by the things made being understood, are plainly seen, both His eternal power and Godhead -- to their being inexcusable" (Romans 1:20). So, we know God exists without His creation. With this knowledge, we have a choice to choose a living God over statues and ones from the imagination. To reiterate, creation indicates the work of God, and denying His existence is inexcusable.

Other false teachings have imposed restrictions on women. During an earlier occasion in college, I ran into a classmate from my hometown. We struck up a very good conversation. Both of us were delighted to share our faith in Christ, until he began to list the restrictions for women. I asked him, then why has God given women knowledge, intelligence and talents, if He did not want women to use them? He could not answer.

Reflecting on that discussion brings to mind the parable of the talents.

The master rebukes his servant, because he buries what he has, rather than making an investment. Let us not bury the unlimited gifts from God that children, women and men have to offer the Church. Also, every time I think about the scripture, that, " '...there is not here male and female...' " (Galatians 3:28), I know God desires believers to work together for His good, maximizing individual capacities for the building of the church body. Together, let us recognize the vessels God chooses, instead of ones to reflect personal appetites, stereotypes, sectarian rules or cultural norms. That way we become one body in and for Christ, reaping dividends from God.

Over the years, I have watched how pastors and other leaders in God's family misused their authority and misinterpreted the Word of God. One particular pastor opposed ordaining women pastors. At a gathering, he asked pastors to come forward. When the women came, he said ordained pastors. Women kept coming, and he said only men. From retirement, he ramped up a full assault against ordaining women and died, soon after. I remember another pastor who fell gravely ill, after he preached that Apostle Paul was only mistaken for an Egyptian, because of the clothing he wore. One should remember the plight of Miriam, who was stricken with leprosy and placed outside of the camp for supplanting the Word of God, spoken by her brother, Moses. Another example was King Herod. He accepted the praise of the people who were claiming that he spoke with the voice of a god and not of a man. As a result, a messenger of the Lord stuck him, worms consumed him and he died (Acts 12:21-23).

The Lord says, "He who is having an ear – let him hear what the Spirit saith to the assemblies: He who is overcoming may not be injured of the second death" (Revelation 2:11). To the Hebrews (9:14) Paul asks, "how much more shall the blood of the Christ (who through the age-during Spirit did offer himself unblemished to God) purify your conscience from dead works to serve the living God?" Jesus has overcome the world (John 16:33), and His blood cleanses sin and purifies the conscience from dead works to serve a living God (Hebrews 10:31). Experiencing this process matures believers to partake of "strong food" allowing them to use senses exercised for the discernment of good from evil (Hebrews 5:14). So, we have the single sacrifice of Christ to cleanse us and our consciences, and by His past work to enter the holy places, once, we have redemption forever

(Hebrews 9:12).

God is supreme and on the throne, showing us to elevate Christ to His rightful position in our hearts and minds. Jesus frees people, and His ascension to His Father shows He sits on His throne, at the right hand of God (See: Romans 8:34 and Hebrews 12:2). Jesus promises, "He who is overcoming – I will give to him to sit with me in my throne, as I also did overcome and did sit down with my Father in His throne" (Revelation 3:21). (For more scriptures describing overcoming, please read: Revelation 2:26; 3:5; 3:12; 3:21.)

Reading the scripture, I Samuel 17:46, shows God positioning David to act against his enemy, to approach and to condemn Goliath. As believers, we must submit ourselves to God and possess boldness to stand against evil. One must "be subject, then, to God; stand up against the devil, and he will flee from you" (James 4:7). Firmly planted "put on the whole armour of God, for your being able to stand against the wiles of the devil" (Ephesians 6:11). We only need to put on our armor once, but put on the whole suit.

With boldness, in John 8:58, Jesus told the Pharisees that he was God, " ' Verily, verily, I say to you, Before Abraham's coming – I am' ". He said to Philip, " '…he who has seen me has seen the Father…' " (John 14:9). God gave us His example of boldness to have, to stand for the truth and to proclaim Christ as the Son of God, God in the flesh, back from the dead. David said of the rising again of Christ "…that his soul was not left to hades, nor did his flesh see corruption" (Acts 2:31). Jesus, both Lord and Christ, seated on the right hand of the throne of the God (Acts 2:30, 34, 36) arose.

Contentment

"not that in respect of want I say [it], for I did learn in the things in which I am – to be content; I have known both to be abased, and I have known to abound; in everything and in all things I have been initiated, both to be full and to be hungry, both to abound and to be in want. For all things I have strength, in Christ's strengthening me..." (Philippians 4:11-13).

Rather than accepting God's word and His will one may superimpose her or his own. What I mean to say is that when someone is dissatisfied with God's choice, he or she may choose another path. By masking God's will with another, for various reasons, reflects a lack of contentment to serve God for His purpose to our benefit. Let us not forget the Israelites in the wilderness, who despised God and grieved Moses for meat. They eventually had meat coming out of their nostrils (Numbers 11:20).

One may say sex before marriage is fine. Unfortunately, God calls fornication a plague (Numbers 25:8). Initially, this seems harmless behavior, but displeases God and results in spiritual and mental brokenness, not to mention physical harm and disease. God gives believers the whole armor as protection to guard the body, soul and spirit. Those putting on this armor are under the influence of the Holy Spirit. They seek holiness and consider their welfare and that of others, knowing God is all they need.

Both Psalm 37 and the book of Job described ways to have contentment. The entire book of Hebrews and Psalm 37 presented a condensed formula for living a life honoring to God. Also, contentment was evident in Job who experienced great distress and catastrophic loss. Not only were his children taken from him in one day, the same day messengers continued to deliver news of his lost herds and substantial riches. Throughout the crippling ordeal, Job blessed the Lord, and waited on God for an answer to the devastation he experienced. Being with Job, at the onset, later his closest friends and even his wife soon turned against him.

Job described his experience as things too wonderful for him to understand (Job 42:3). Unable to blame God for his sorrow he prayed for his friends, instead. This showed the contentment Job had for God. Having mourned the death of his children, Job remained anchored in the Lord. After Job's ordeal the Mighty God continued to bless him with children, multiplied his former wealth, admonished his friends and instructed them to take gifts to him (Job 42).

Like Job others faced hardships. After God removed Saul as king, He raised up David: "…He did raise up to them David for king, to whom also having testified, he [God] said, I found David, the son of Jesse, a man according to My heart, who shall do all My will" (Acts 13:22). David stayed true to God and accomplished the tasks God gave him. He suffered loss and remained resolute to walk with God. Even after God refused to heal his first son with Bathsheba, David followed God and shepherded His people. Turning to God for guidance, David praised Him through Psalms. Full of contentment, David chose punishment from God for numbering the troops. David also passed on the plans to build the temple to his son, Solomon (I Chronicles 22:6).

For our benefit, we must pray as David, "Keep me as the apple, the daughter of the eye, In the shadow of Thy wings thou dost hide me" (Psalm 17:8). This sentiment also appeared in Deuteronomy 32:10, "…He keepeth him [Israel] as the apple of His eye". So, become

CONTENTMENT

blameless and harmless by working without complaining, whining, having a bad temper and disputing. Move close enough to God for your reflection to be seen in His pupils. (See: http://rzim.org/just-a-thought-broadcasts/the-apple-of-his-eye/). Also, Paul writes, " All things do without murmurings and reasonings, that ye may become blameless and harmless, children of God, unblemished in the midst of a generation crooked and perverse, among whom ye do appear as luminaries in the world..." (Philippians 2:14-15).

Possessing contentment to do the will of the Lord has been a struggle for me. Raised to be self-sufficient and an independent thinker has led to a life of both failures and successes. Thankfully, I stayed focused in school and reaped the benefits of good grades and college degrees. However, having read Ecclesiastes, again, illuminated the vanity in everything. Those good grades, degrees, treasures, awards, accolades and societies were nothing in relation to living right for God.

As a business owner, I have heard questions such as: "What have you done for me, lately?" Well, what have you done for God, lately? Growth acquired from strategic transitions may quickly disappear. Shortcutting the process for exceptional wealth, with unethical practices, financial or otherwise, has caused untold damage to businesses and to consumers. Accomplishing goals through methods rooted in greed have proven to be the vehicles for failure.

A solution to combat these temptations is intercessory prayer. This is my best defense and offense (Acts 3:20). Know that the Spirit intercedes (Romans 8:27), and Jesus does, too (Romans 8:34). "Seek ye Jehovah, while He is found. Call ye Him, while He is near" (Isaiah 55:6). So, let us pray for one another and keep our thoughts toward fellow believers struggling to honor Christ in a hostile environment toward Him. Pray for one another to have the life of the Spirit that gives life to the body, like the body of our Lord Jesus (Romans 8:11).

We must also pray for ourselves. Once, my mother had about five bleeding ulcers. The doctor concluded that her only option was to remove portions of her stomach. Mom told me the night before the doctor's visit, to discuss the surgery, how she cried out to the Lord to keep her stomach intact. The day my mother went to the doctor, he couldn't find any more ulcers. Praise God.

THE CONSCIENCE OF GOD

On my journey to serve the Lord, I have explored many ways to have contentment coupled with faith. Years ago, I prayed and anointed my children with oil. Honestly, it was for me too. If God blessed them, then I would feel confident that I was going to make it through the day without declaring war on the entire household. No longer desiring to pray with handkerchiefs from a variety of ministries, that always got dirty at the bottom of my purse, I felt compelled to buy a tallit or prayer shawl. I always wanted a tallit, and years ago I purchased one. A Prophet was offering them for an exorbitant donation, but I gave it any way. My hope was that the money was used to build God's kingdom. Later, I bought another one for my daughter, from another ministry.

The tallit possesses no intrinsic power. I pray under it. God meets me there and hears my prayers to help the sick, both physically and spiritually. I look at the stripes and think about the beating Jesus took for me. I touch the tassels and ponder the healing power of God.

One morning before dawn, God sent an angel to wake me. I felt something rocking my hips. Yes, God was saying get up and pray. Other times, I prayed to have a full nights rest. I found it best to wake up early and pray to set the stage for the recipients of my prayers and my day. Usually at that time I haven't eaten, so while fasting, this has been a prime time to pray against demonic activity.

Another time my mom was at the hospital recovering from a stroke. She was so sick that she began uttering unintelligible phrases. I went home, got my tallit and began praying with her under it. In a few minutes, she was talking to me and calling my name. My sister, who was sitting by our mother's bed said, "Keep doing that."

Again, prayer and oil have been instrumental and powerfully effective for healing. Being diabetic, my mother had developed what the doctors thought was an infection in her foot. Previous surgery to remove pieces of bone and tissue from mom's toes and the top of her foot failed to alleviate the problem. At the time, mom was on the second most potent antibiotic. Mom's doctors feared that if she was prescribed the most potent one, and it didn't work, that she might be in greater danger.

Well, eventually, mom went to a tropical fungus specialist and received

CONTENTMENT

the proper diagnosis. In fact, a tropical fungus was growing in her foot. Being an avid gardener throughout our travels abroad, mom had contracted this fungus that presented itself many years later. The fungus continued to grow and she was prescribed a different regimen that failed, as well. Some time went by and mom called to tell me the doctors were considering amputation.

With the news from my mother that her foot may be amputated, I began to pray and called out to the Lord for an answer. He told me to anoint her foot and to pray for her. Well, I was hesitant and very reluctant to tell my mother that I was commissioned to pray for her. So, a few days before I anointed my mother's foot, I told her that I was going to pray for her. As was uncustomary for mom she didn't respond, but only had a funny expression on her face. When I told her that I was going to pray for her again, she kind of smiled.

The day finally came and I told mom that I was coming to pray for her. She agreed and said that she was going to humor me. Mom sat down on her extra dining room chair and I anointed my hands. I told her to lift up her foot. She said that she couldn't. When I helped her lift her foot and it went over her head. Mom and I looked on in amazement, because mom could never lift her foot very high. The Lord said, "Slap the top of her foot." I questioned God and told Him that I would hurt her. I relented and told Him that He had to guide my hand. When my hand hit the top of mom's foot we heard this cracking sound. After a while it stopped and I put mom's foot down.

That same week all of the swelling went down in mom's foot. The other foot remained swollen and the healed foot stayed normal. I told mom that I would pray for the other foot, but she wasn't inclined to have any more prayer. God received the glory, because my mom kept her foot and the examination by the doctor showed a clear x-ray, and no more fungus was ever found in mom's foot, again. The pervasive thought among other family members was that the medicine had started working. I responded by asking, "Why, then, were the doctors going to amputate mom's foot?" God be praised.

My mother taught me to honor God and to keep His name holy. God's hand worked wonderful miracles in my mother's life. Consistently, my mother honored and loved God. She had a remarkable testimony of how good Jesus was to her. How God blessed me with her.

Before mom died she was gravely ill and required round the clock medical care. Due to several strokes, Mom was in and out of the hospital, a rehabilitation facility and nursing care. She always kept up a good spirit and was eager to make you smile. So, when the nurses told me that her test results were those of a dead person, I was heart broken. They couldn't explain why she was still alive. This was the second to last nursing home for mom and God instructed me to leave my tallit on her bed. In turn, I informed all of the staff to replace the tallit on her bed, after changing her linen. The doctors didn't know what was wrong with mom, but God was merciful and my mom came out of her dreadful state to celebrate her seventieth birthday with us.

I remember how saddened my mom was when she saw that her blood stained my tallit. I felt reassured by God that it would be all right. So, I told mom not to worry and that it would be okay. In God's faithfulness the stains all washed away.

Mom was moved to another nursing home. As I was leaving, I reached to place my tallit on her bed, but the Lord wouldn't direct me to do so. I kept trying to take the tallit out of the closet to place it on mom's bed, but I couldn't. Finally, I turned to mom and said to her, "I guess you don't need it anymore". I smiled at my mom and went back to kiss her, once more. Her face was swollen from another stroke and she looked so tired. I just couldn't seem to go.

That Saturday morning mom passed away. Truly, the contentment mom possessed was from the Lord and evident in her walk with the Him. Her service to Jesus marked her courage to defy the hardships. Through all of her misery and many sicknesses, mom never blamed God, but chose rather to speak about the Lord's works, and of His goodness.

Let us possess a reverence for God and be satisfied in Him. May we continue to know, "Without covetousness the behaviour, being content with the things present, for He hath said, 'No, I will not leave, no, nor forsake thee' " (Hebrews 13:5). I Timothy 6:6 tells us "but it is great gain — the piety with contentment".

Humility

"… be made low before the Lord, and He shall exalt you" (James 4:10).

No matter how wretched and wicked one has been, God saw the heart and potential. The Bible told how David, on many occasions, abused his power and repeatedly repented. Psalm 51 recounted how David humbled himself before the Lord. Making many mistakes, David ordered Joab to number the troops; sent for Bathsheba, a married woman he saw bathing, impregnated, and then orchestrated the death of her husband, Uriah. Matthew even mentioned Bathsheba's former husband, Uriah, in chapter 1, verse 6. Despite his failings, David called on the Lord and turned from his unrighteousness.

So, the answer to the question: Do we sin knowing that God has to forgive us? Well, God is not mocked. Remember the scripture, "Be not led astray; God is not mocked; for what a man may sow – that also he shall reap, because he who is sowing to his own flesh, of the flesh shall reap corruption; and he who is sowing to the Spirit, of the Spirit shall reap life age-during…" (Galatians 6:7 and 8). That is why sin leads to death, because we are doing what we want and not what God wants. Sowing to the flesh leads to corruption. Let us sow to the Spirit, and live.

Helping another person has rewards and may even feel satisfying. Though admirable, if the glory is kept and none goes to God, the work is in vain. What does that mean? If you are working to fulfill your needs and others without honoring God, then that is all you will gain. Consequently, the one you seek to please may be unappreciative. Do you seek to please others just to have them throw it back in your face? God never does that, because He honors those who seek to please Him.

Have humility while serving the Lord. When you fulfill His needs, as God requires, then He will reward you. Just like Cain, you and I have the choice to do well and receive acceptance from God, or not and have a "...sin-offering [that] is crouching…" (Genesis 4:7).

No longer should one rely on the praise, and admiration of others, because God becomes the debtor to receive the glory for them. " 'And the king answering, shall say to them, Verily I say to you, Inasmuch as ye did [it] to one of these my brethren – the least – to me ye did [it]" (Matthew 25:40).

When Jehovah caused the incurable sickness of David and Bathsheba's son (I Samuel 2:15), David fasted and prayed to no avail. As devastating as it was, that decision to kill the child was one only God could have made. God knew His plans had to be fulfilled at any cost. Unfortunately, the incident with Uriah caused God's enemies to blaspheme Him. God conveyed His disdain for the resulting contempt that His enemies had for Him. He forgave David's sin and spared his life, but His Word remained and the son died. As mentioned earlier, David tried to cover up the adultery by killing Bathsheba's husband, Uriah. Upon his son's death, David immediately rose up, stopped weeping and fasting and went on with life, because his sacrifice unto death was insufficient to save his child.

Too often living to please oneself is a source of the greatest pain, conflict and emptiness. This is the harsh reality for interfering with God's plans and emboldening His enemies. However, after reaching one's end, there still is hope. A person truly repentant in heart and willing to make a change, just like David and even Nebuchanezzer, may rise to his or her greatest potential. There is a Living God who lovingly restores relationships, heals souls, spirits and bodies. All other gods lack this ability. Turn to the Word, Jesus and fall at His feet having humility to enable Him to start the process of spiritual cleansing and change.

Accepting the decisions of God, and abasing our predilections for sinning, honor God and represent true humility. This is why God corrects those He loves and exalts the humble. Further, the righteousness of God is present through a walk of faith. Conversely, He pours His wrath out to those concealing the truth. They know what God expects and choose to obscure the works of God. Rather than giving God thanks and praise, they turn against Him, corrupting His message. When one overrules God's standards, he or she acts in His place. For declaring man and animals as gods, God "gave [gives] them up to dishonorable affections" (Romans 1: 26).

Others, however, such as King Nebuchadnezzar, by God's mercy and grace, reached both the lowest point and highest. After an episode of mental instability, a devastating physical transformation and a steady diet of herb, eaten by oxen, King Nebuchadnezzar regained his mind and was able to return to his former state. Becoming a believer in God and His authority, King Nebuchadnezzar blessed, praised and honored God (Daniel 4:34, 37). Not only did God restore the king, He also increased his greatness. Thankfully, the Sovereignty of God stood, then and now, to continue to the ages.

With humility embrace the joy that God's law is final (Psalm 1:2). On our own, we have neither the resources nor the capacity to remove sin. The law of God is the conductor showing us the way to live, leading to Jesus and righteousness (Galatians 3:24). The Old and New Testaments define following God's laws. In particular, Matthew 5 indicates that any one teaching the removal of even the smallest part of the commandments will be least in the Kingdom. Why? Jesus is the fulfillment of the law (Matthew 5:17) and every part of the law is present in Christ. Christ brings forgiveness and the final sacrifice for sin, making the Law complete. This renders other sacrifices for sin worthless. Being good does not get you to Heaven. 1 John 2:2 reads, "and he -- he is a propitiation for our sins, and not for ours only, but also for the whole world...." We don't need to pay for our sins. Jesus' death is the only worthy offering to substitute our payment due for sin and free us from a certain place in Hell. Also, read: I Peter 2:23.

So, do we stone or pay an eye for an eye? No, because vengeance belongs to the Lord. Hebrews 10:30 states "for we have known Him who is saying, 'Vengeance [is] Mine, I will recompense, saith the Lord;' " and again, 'The Lord shall judge His people;' ". One who commits sin dies spiritually. That person gives himself or herself to serve the flesh and not God. In essence, they die by committing spiritual suicide.

In Matthew 23, Jesus tells the people and His disciples to follow the teaching of the Pharisees and the Scribes, but not to imitate their behavior. Jesus delivers a scathing rebuke to the Scribes and Pharisees for burdening the people with heavy, grievous tasks without lifting a finger to help them. They obstruct people from going to heaven; take advantage of widows, and travel to find followers only to make them more deceptive than themselves. Also, these religious leaders do not gain access to enter in to the heavens. Even though they pay tithes, they overlook the heavier assignments of the law: "…the judgment, and the kindness, and the faith; these it behoved [you] to do and those not to neglect" (Matthew 23:23).

In the Bible sin was paid for with physical punishment. For this reason, Jesus suffered in His flesh and died to satisfy the payment for our sin. Now, the New Testament commandments have taught us how to live under the Old Testament commandments as evidenced in Christ's teachings. We were instructed to sow to the Spirit. Furthermore, Jesus taught His disciples to correct sinners and to forgive a brother as often as he reconsidered or changed his thoughts about his behavior (Luke 17:3). Forgive as your brother or sister asks and needs to be forgiven.

Possessing humility by disowning ourselves, we follow God's law to pick up our crosses daily (Luke 9:23). John 12:25 states, " he who is loving his life shall lose it, and he who is hating his life in this world – to life age-during shall keep it". To live without being self-serving means we must have the desire to please God. So, the righteous continues living eternally, whereas the unrighteous loses the gift of life.

Unfortunately, individuals, such as the rich man who refused to help poor Lazarus, will be tormented forever. Lazarus had been placed at the gate, to beg. Even the dogs sought to comfort Lazarus who was routinely ignored by the rich man. Likewise, in Genesis, after Joseph's brothers had thrown him into the pit they dismissed his cries (Genesis 37:20-24 and Genesis 42:21). Thankfully, Joseph's fate was part of God's plan to save multitudes of people. The brothers' chance for redemption and forgiveness showed God's mercy. Unfortunately, the self-absorbed rich man's heart was too seared to change. Even in Hades, he commanded Abraham to send Lazarus to fetch some water. In his depravity, the rich man refused to see Lazarus' value came from God, who made us all in His image.

We know from John 6:44 that the Father draws a person to Christ. I firmly believe that this method and process toward salvation remains consistent, today. The Father, through His commandments, guides us to make worthy decisions and prepares us to receive salvation. Jesus gives us the law to recognize sin (Romans 7:7). So, now we know, all religions do not lead to God. Having a Godly standard with humility makes way for the miraculous transformation of salvation and regeneration. Once we die, we no longer have the option to receive the life Christ offers. Now, not tomorrow, but now, we must with humility, accept the gift Jesus offers us. Let us be like the thief on the cross with contentment to honor the Lord, boldness to speak up for Christ, zeal to abandon sin, faith to know our place is with Jesus and humility to petition His favor. Will you ask Jesus to forgive you? It is that simple. Ask, "Jesus, forgive me?"

Embracing God's will and his righteous decisions show submission to God. By following the teachings of Christ and His righteousness, a believer in Christ experiences His peace. Therefore, living a life pleasing to the Lord and accomplishing His purpose, according to the Bible, gives a believer the perfect example to follow. Let us put away all matters of evil and with humility embrace God's engrafted Word that is able to save our souls (James 1:21).

So, receiving Jesus' gift of forgiveness grants our spirits and souls eternal life. Through His death and resurrection, Christ of the New Testament, gives life to the sinner. Christ's blood sacrifice and broken body, replaces every person's debt for sin from Adam. If we desire to live eternally in Heaven, then valuing and embracing Jesus' offering is essential. This directs us to the need for salvation and to live life for Christ now and continually.

In order to by-pass the judgment of the second death or Hell, the Father must see Jesus rather than our sin. Jesus provides a shield for the repentant sinner to block the punishment. This is akin to a family member who rescues the unruly child from the wrath of the mother or the father. If the child continues to misbehave, forgiveness is present along with punishment. Like the child's savior, Jesus saves all who come to Him with humility in their hearts.

With humility we must honor God for making us in His image. Father, Son and Spirit comprise the three parts of the living God. Being in God's image (Genesis 1:27), we also have three parts. The body, soul and spirit represent the whole person (I Thessalonians 5:23). Although we may let the peace of Jesus Christ guard our hearts and minds, we have the unique ability to think on what we hope to obtain. Writing to the Philippians, Apostle Paul told them to think on things of worth and praise, being true, righteous, grave (venerable), lovely, and of a good report (Philippians 4:8).

Jesus submitted to His Father, and showed His love for all humanity to suffer humiliation, pain and separation from His Father. God the Father facilitated the maturation of His plan for salvation and severed Himself from Jesus. God, the Father did not die for our sin, nor became sin, because apart from Jesus, the flesh was unavailable to take the sin. Thus the Father had to remove Himself and to abandon His Son, in order for the sacrifice to be made. He left Jesus to take the punishment for us, and to give us righteousness (II Corinthians 5:21).

Submitted to His Father's will, "Jesus cried out with a great voice, saying, 'Eli, Eli, lama sabachthani?' That is, 'My God, my God, why didst Thou forsake me?' " (Matthew 27:46). Jesus spoke to a Father, who had entrusted Him with complete confidence to complete His task, alone. Knowing Hell was the consequence for sin, at the cross, Jesus had faith for deliverance and released His Spirit into the Father's hands. If Jesus had sinned, He would have been trapped in death to face judgment in Hell. Jesus' endurance set the standard for winning and without Him it is impossible to do. Just like Paul, as believers, we have been "looking to the author and perfecter of faith – Jesus, who, over-against the joy set before him – did endure a cross, shame having despised, on the right hand also of the throne of God did sit down" (Hebrews 12:2).

After living a perfect life without sin and always having His Father with Him, Jesus now was asked to do two things He had never done: to be forsaken by the Father (Matthew 27:26) and succumb to the shame of becoming sin (Hebrews 12:2; II Corinthians 5:21). Becoming sin would cause a separation from His Father. I believe the separation and the public humiliation of sin were the things in the cup that Jesus didn't want to drink. Similar to the cup described earlier, that was dipped into the ocean and filled with blasphemy and idolatry.

Faced with the dilemma, Jesus passionately pleaded with His Father in the Garden of Gethsemane. As God's Son, Jesus knew He had to die to fulfill the law and to release all from the curse of the law. Having the keys to death (eternal death without God, the state) and Hades (the place), Jesus' death separated His Spirit from His body and released God's power for all to overcome physical and spiritual death. This was apparent at Jesus' death when the tombs opened and many bodies of the saints, after Christ's soul, arose and appeared to a number of people in the holy city (Matthew 27:52-53).

In both the New and Old Testaments the Law of God required punishment for sin. In the Old Testament, God dispossessed from His presence those who committed abominations "…causing his son and his daughter to pass over into fire, a user of divinations, an observer of clouds, and an enchanter, and a sorcerer, and a charmer, and one asking at a familiar spirit, and a wizard, and one seeking unto the dead" (Deuteronomy 18:10-11). In Jeremiah 7: 31-32, the people of Judah built altars to burn their sons and daughters, and as a result were to be slaughtered, leaving no place to bury the dead. Also, Saul expelled those with familiar spirits and wizards from the land (I Samuel 28:3). With regard to the content of God's Law, that was never abandoned, consequences for sin remained from the Old to the New Testaments. However, the treatment of the offender changed with the teachings of Christ, and Jesus became the final sacrifice for sin. So, Jesus did not come to abolish, but to fulfill the Law (Matthew 5:17).

The shadows of the Old Testament, the prophecies, were manifested in the New Testament. Jesus addressed the falsehood of doing away with the commandments in Matthew chapter 5, verses 17 through 19: " 'Do not suppose that I came to throw down the law or the prophets – I did not come to throw down, but to fulfil; for, verily I say to you, till that the heaven and the earth may pass away, one iota or one tittle may not pass away from the law, till that all may come to pass. 'Whoever therefore may loose one of these commands – the least –and may teach men so, least he shall be called in the reign of the heavens, but whoever may do and may teach [them], he shall be called great in the reign of the heavens."

Jesus continued to uphold the commands and statutes. However, by Jesus' command, God's children discontinued enforcing the punishments, because God ordered love in the believers' hearts. God's children no longer imposed the sentence of "an eye for an eye, and tooth for tooth" (Matthew 5:38). Jesus reinforced the teaching of inwardly governing spiritual laws given to the Jews in Jeremiah and again in Hebrews by placing His laws on our hearts and in our minds:

> "For this is the covenant that I make, With the house of Israel, after those days, An affirmation of Jehovah, I have given My law in their inward part, And on their heart I do write it, And I have been to them for God, And they are to me for a people" (Jeremiah 31:31).

> " 'This [is] the covenant that I will make with them after those days, saith the Lord, giving My laws on their hearts, and upon their minds I will write them' " (Hebrews 10:16).

Now, we have been offered this opportunity to show the world we belong to God by loving as Jesus loved:

> " 'A new commandment I give to you, that ye love one another; according as I did love you, that ye also love one another; in this shall all know that ye are my disciples, if ye may have love one to another' " (John 13:34-35).

So, it is not a light thing to distort the Word of God. The shadow, in the Old Testament customs and Law, points to coming things and God's perfecting power through Christ (Hebrews 10:1; Colossians 2:16-17). Christ's love provides the long awaited liberation of women and the abolishment of the abusive practices of ancient cultures and traditions. Believers have liberty in Christ to live as kings and priests. Jews and non-Jews unite into one new being. God breaks the barriers of nationality, ethnicity, class, and gender. Adam or mankind, being male and female (Genesis 5:2), is reborn in Christ. What a revelation.

God establishes an order to depict the relationship of Christ to the Church. God, as our boss, is fitting us together in love (Ephesians 4:16), and presents His wife unblemished (Ephesians 5:27). Husbands and wives are positions. Let us not equate this with male domination and female submission. As a servant, Jesus washes his disciples' feet. He feeds them on the shore. He prays, teaches, and protects His loved ones. Doing all to the glory of the Father, Jesus with humility obeys and submits to the will of God. Those are the kinds of husbands God wants for His daughters and wives for His sons.

God's plans prevailed over the lives of Abram and Sarai, Hannah and Elkanah, Ruth and Boaz, David and Bathsheba, Joseph and Mary. God told Abram to leave his people, his land and his father's house to go to an unknown place (Genesis 12:1). Sarai conceived at ninety to have Isaac (Genesis 17:17). God granted Hannah her prayer and gave her a son. She then told her husband, Elkanah, she was going to take their son before the face of Jehovah for him to live there (I Samuel 1:22-23). Ruth was a Moabite. Moab was the incestuous child of Lot with his eldest daughter (Genesis 19:37). As we know, Mary was betrothed and pregnant, by the Holy Spirit, with Jesus. Before the wedding, Joseph was going to discreetly sever his commitment to her (Matt. 1:19), but God prevailed. Abraham (Abram), Sarah (Sarai), Ruth, Boaz, David, Bathsheba and Mary were all in the lineage of Jesus, the Messiah.

If a husband cannot affirm that he has been given an instruction from God, he should never ask his wife to follow him. Likewise, the wife must seek the Lord to help and encourage her husband in the Lord. Once God told me to ask my former husband, if He/God had given him certain instructions for me to follow. My ex-husband labored to answer. As he was forming his mouth to answer in the affirmative, a presence was filling the room that made both of us very afraid. I actually stepped away from him. Thankfully, he valued his life and eventually answered truthfully and said, "No".

In order to serve God, studying or being diligent to know the Word of God and to follow God's leading is critical for a husband and a wife. To maintain a steady course, each spouse must be vigilant to nurture his and her individual walk with God. It is the role of the husband to provide love, exemplifying Christ to the wife. The wife has an obligation to follow her husband's Godly direction, because the "…assembly is subject to Christ, so also the wives to their own husbands in everything" (Ephesians 5:24). Everything subject to God's will. Make no mistake, God tells the wife and the husband to refuse ungodliness. Together the husband and the wife acknowledge and follow the Lord. However, a husband cannot lead a wife who is overbearing and refuses to follow God. Likewise a wife cannot serve with a husband who refuses to obey God's will. In the fear of the Lord, men and women must submit, one to the other (Galatians 5:21), and cherish Godly authority.

We are able to operate fully, as the body of Christ with humility, in the capacities that God designates. Just as God wants husbands and wives to be one, He wants all who believe in Him to be of "one body and one Spirit, according as also ye were called in one hope of your calling" (Ephesians 4:4). It is time for all believers in Christ to unite. We must lay aside divisions. Jesus calls those who are burdened and He will give them rest (Matthew 11:28). He says take His yoke and learn from Him, because he is "… meek and humble in heart…" and He will give our souls rest (Matthew 11:29). As believers we should take His yoke and burden, because His yoke is easy and His burden is light (Matthew 11:30).

With thriving ministries at stake God is going to ultimately prevail. It is vitally important to welcome the gifts and callings to come forth for the maturity of all believers. His Godly weapons supply believers with the armaments necessary to destroy strongholds (II Corinthians 10:4). Jesus warns His disciples not to quench the Spirit of God (I Thessalonians 5:19). This hinders unbelievers and stifles the saints. That is why we must know that, " 'With men this is impossible, but with God all things are possible' " (Matthew 19:26).

The Bible has detailed severe consequences for sin, particularly living outside the will of God and harming His people. When the Israelites continued to serve false gods, God allowed their enemy, the Canaanites, to oppress them for twenty years. Fortunately, the reign of Jabin, the Cananite King, came to an end when the Israelites rose up against him. Except for Sisera, his commander, who exited his chariot and fled on foot, all of Jabin's men were lost in battle. Seeking shelter in the home of Jael, wife of Heber the Kenite, Sisera met his end at the hands of a woman. Just as prophesied by Deborah the inspired woman of God and judge of Israel (Judges 4:9 and 4:21).

The book of Amos outlines a host of offenses toward God from brethren killing one another, ripping up pregnant women to increase borders, a father and son defiling the same girl to defame God's name, treading on the needy, buying the poor and selling them for a pair of sandals to the pride of Jacob, whom God almost annihilates (Amos 1:9, 11, 13; 2:7; 7:9 and 8:6). The abysmal perpetual wretchedness in the book of Amos is happening today around the world with the slaughter, mutilation and rape of women, children and men refusing to denounce Christ, along with the torture of others. In Amos 4:6-13, mercifully, God brings cataclysmic events on the earth and death to discourage wickedness and drive people to Him, but the people refuse to relent.

Finally coming together, Ephesians chapter 5 and Matthew chapter 18 reveal the power of believers working to serve God. When there are two or more working in unison to serve the Lord, submitting to one another in the fear of the Lord, a blessed force from God results. Marriage should exemplify a relationship between Christ and the Church. Paul tells us, "this secret is great, and I speak in regard to Christ and to the assembly" (Ephesians 5:32) Paul is referring to available power through service and obedience to God. Matthew chapter 18 shows, in vivid detail, the steps to take when a believer sins against another. First, the offended party must go to the offender personally, to show him/her the fault, in order to win over the person. If unsuccessful, then go again taking one or two as witnesses. Finally, if the person refuses to hear them, go to the assembly. If the person refuses to hear the assembly treat the person as "the heathen and tax-gatherer" (Matthew 18:17).

As a Body of Christ, the authority given by God has power both here and in Heaven. When two or three agree in the Lord, that determination is final on Earth and in Heaven. God the Father grants the petitions of His children acting in the name of His Son, Jesus (Matthew 18:19-20). This is the power of the assembly: " 'Verily I say to you, Whatever things ye may bind upon the earth shall be having been bound in the heavens, and whatever things ye may loose on the earth shall be having been loosed in the heavens. 'Again, I say to you, that, if two of you may agree on the earth concerning anything, whatever they may ask -- it shall be done to them from my Father who is in the heavens, for where there are two or three gathered together – to my name, there am I in the midst of them' " (Matthew 18:18-20).

Revealing the fault of a believer and responding to the complaint of the violated person, as God demands, are acts of love. The Word or Jesus provides the matrix to build-up the Church. This unifies believers and gives the Church the power to petition God, and enables God to grant requests.

We must rebuke and disregard asking for selfish gain. In Matthew 18, Jesus tells His disciples to be as the little one to enter into the reign of the heavens. Being as one of God's little ones in Christ is a bond of perfection. Those believing in Christ and walking together in the service of the Lord command and possess the power to bind and loose on the earth and it will be done in the heavens.

The friendship between Jonathan and David illustrated a true brotherly bond of (II Samuel 1:26). According to God's plan, Jonathan relinquished his claim to the throne for David. As God's anointed (I Samuel 16:13), David was destined to be king. After making a covenant, Jonathan persevered to help David. While God kept Saul from finding David (I Samuel 23:14), Jonathan's actions solidified a formidable bond between dear friends. Upon Jonathan's death, David said Jonathan's love for him surpassed the love of women (II Samuel 1:26). Their covenant to one another was kept unto death, as a union of the soul (I Samuel 18:1-5; 20:11, 42).

Just like David and Jonathan, believers are to submit to one another, "…but in humility of mind one another counting more excellent than yourselves – each not to your own look ye, but each also to the things of others" (Philippians 2:3 and 4). Remember Christ gave himself as a servant of God and was highly exalted. Christ did not count it robbery to be equal with God and yet came as a servant to God in the form of God and man (Philippians 2: 6 and 7). God then, gave Him a name above every name (Philippians 2:9). So, when we submit to one another, putting others first, we show the humility we have and a mind of Christ. In like manner, both the husband and the wife are working for the same good, to please God and to fulfill His calling.

Winning others for Christ is our harvest or our fruit. Also, the fruit of the Spirit come from knowing; therefore, trusting and consequently following Jesus Christ. Bear fruit as Jesus tells us in John chapter 15 verses 1-2, " 'I am the true vine, and my Father is the husbandman; every branch in me not bearing fruit, He doth take it away, and every one bearing fruit, He doth cleanse by pruning it, that it may bear more fruit…' " Also, in verse four, "…remain in me, and I in you, as the branch is not able to bear fruit of itself, if it may not remain in the vine, so neither ye, if ye may not remain in me."

So, the unfruitful are unable to remain in Jesus. Consequently death will ensue, but remaining in Christ bears fruit. " 'I am the vine, ye the branches; he who is remaining in me, and I in him, this one doth bear much fruit, because apart from me ye are not able to do anything; if any one may not remain in me, he was cast forth without as the branch, and was withered, and they gather them, and cast to fire, and they are burned; if ye may remain in me, and my sayings in you may remain, whatever ye may wish ye shall ask, and it shall be done to you" (John 15:5-7).

How do you ask in Jesus' name? Here is how: "if ye may remain in me, and my sayings in you may remain, whatever ye may wish ye shall ask and it shall be done to you" (John 15:7). Also, see John chapter 18. Loosing and binding what is in Heaven and on the Earth depends on our relationship with God and other believers. So, then, " 'Ye did not choose out me, but I chose out you, and did appoint you, that ye might go away, and might bear fruit, and your fruit might remain, that whatever ye may ask of the Father in my name, He may give you" (John 15:16). You must bear fruit, remain in Jesus, and then you may ask what you wish. That is asking in Jesus' name. Bearing fruit by loving one another shows God's Spirit dwells in the believer and they remain in God (I John 4:11-14). One also remains in God by acknowledging Jesus as God's Son (I John 4:15).

Those who stumble refuse to give up their lives to Christ, to bear the fruit of the Spirit. By neglecting to serve others and love souls for Christ, many relinquish their ability to act as Christ does to bear fruit.

Thus they sow to the flesh, reaping corruption and not to the Spirit reaping life age-during. Notice the scripture, Galatians 6:8, exemplifies this: "because he who is sowing to his own flesh, of the flesh shall reap corruption; and he who is sowing to the Spirit, of the Sprit shall reap life age-during...."

To labor for God resulted in life eternally and having chosen this option prevented stumbling. In John 15, Jesus prepared His disciples to face opposition. He stressed to them that His works fulfilled the word, but caused those who hated Him to sin. Hating both Jesus and His Father, Jesus' enemies despised Him without a cause. With the departure of Christ, the Holy Spirit came from the Father to testify of Him along with the disciples. Jesus concluded and said, " 'These things I have spoken to you, that ye may not be stumbled" (John 16:1).

God gave these warnings to help all believers to produce fruit. I Samuel 28 and I Chronicles 10:13-14 showed how God judged Saul for his disobedience. The Prophet Samuel gave very specific instructions from God to Saul. Saul refused to wait for Samuel and made the sacrifice in defiance to God. Also, Saul refused to abandon the spoils of the enemy. Again, Saul violated God's command to kill the king he defeated. For defying God, to follow his own will and fearing the people, God striped Saul of his kingship. Further, Saul turned to the witch of Endor to conjure Samuel's spirit for an audience. The witch, of course, was unable to raise Samuel. God sent Samuel to deliver a message to Saul and prophesied of his death along with his sons.

Disobedience to God stops fruitfulness and maturation in Christ. With humility serving God faithfully, without lip service, produces great gains for Christ. Consequently, many die who take of the cup unworthily. God signifies His unwillingness to allow individuals the reign in His body who misrepresent Him and pretend to be His children. So, it is essential to follow God and lead others to God. Depending on Christ to bear fruit, believers know apart from Jesus they " 'are not able to do anything...' " (John 15:5).

John says, " 'For I testify to every one hearing the words of the prophecy of this scroll, if any one may add unto these, God shall add to him the plagues that have been written in this scroll, and if any one may take away from the words of the scroll of this prophecy, God shall take away his part from the scroll of the life, and out of the holy city, and the things that have been written in this scroll….' " (Revelation 22:18-19).

How wonderful it is to know that God saves from the horror that dwells within and without this life, the one after. I give praise to God for preserving my life, delivering me from the mistakes that I have made, and saving me from Hell and the second death (Revelation 20:14-15). With humility, I pray that the words of this book echo God's Word. The fear of the Lord, keep me in step with His will, and abiding in His presence.

"In like manner, ye younger, be subject to elders, and all to one another subjecting yourselves; with humble-mindedness clothe yourselves, because God the proud doth resist, but to the humble He doth give grace; be humbled, then, under the powerful hand of God, that you He may exalt in good time all your care having cast upon Him, because He careth for you" (1 Peter 5:5-7).

Faith

"And faith is of things hoped for a confidence, of matters not seen a conviction" (Hebrews 11:1). "... According to the abundance of His kindness did beget us again to a living hope, through the rising again of Jesus Christ out of the dead (I Peter 1:3). Faith is a gift from God and not of ourselves that we may boast (Ephesians 2:8-9).

2011
Now, as I am writing this, I have been diagnosed with grade two, stage three invasive lobular carcinoma. I have a surgically implanted port in my left chest subclavical area. The reliance on healthy eating did not save me from getting cancer. I have been convinced that had I not been so committed over the years to eating a healthy diet, that I would not have the strong immune system necessary to withstand the chemotherapy and the Neulasta shot. My body is shutting down and the organs seem to want to fail. This treatment is very devastating to my once strong and resilient body. God will get the glory from all of this, because He said to me that the treatment would kill me, but He would restore me. How glad I will be when God breathes life into me and I am cancer free.

This cancer has been a blow to my time and comfort. The treatment is painful and tiring. The first chemo treatment I had, backed-up into my sinuses and drained for two weeks into my mouth. The first Neulasta (pegfilgrastim) shot made me feel as though I was having a mild heart attack and gave me terrible pains in my bones. I had a pain that started in my chest went down my left arm, up my throat and came around into my back. After the second episode of this same pain, following the same path, I called the doctor. The next day the Nurse Practitioner told me I was doing quite well with the treatment. If that was doing well, I hated to see the poor slob who had a rough time.

The Lord may make my enemies my footstool. He has my permission to send them to the side of the pit. Yes, chain them up in the pit of Hell. Often, I feel as though I am going to die. The enemies buffet me with taunts of dismay, but my faith says that God is stronger than death itself. All of my intercessors have been praying for me and sending me scripture. Satan has tried everything to stop me from fulfilling God's call in my life. He has really made great efforts to discourage me, but I will win.

Diet is a factor and I must continue to eat healthily. Within five months, the oncologist foresees me losing my right breast and the cancerous lymph nodes under my right arm. This sickness is for God's glory and I am convinced that I serve a victor and not a victim. Just tonight, God showed me: Hebrews 1:13 and 14, "And unto which of the messengers said He ever, 'Sit at My right hand, till I may make thine enemies thy footstool?' are they not all spirits of service – for ministration being sent forth because of those about to inherit salvation?"

Just this morning, Sunday, August 14, 2011, God showed me how to use any scripture to encourage myself. For example, "Jesus wept", (John 11:35) showed His love for us. Also, the scripture from Hebrews 1:5, " 'My Son thou art – I to-day have begotten thee?' " revealed the power of God and His mercy to send our Salvation.

As one of my Bible Study Fellowship sisters pointed out, this illness is for God's glory. He is using it to make our enemies our footstools for those about to inherit salvation. My friends, clients and acquaintances prayed for me. Through this illness, God was bringing Salvation to my family and those around me.

Looking back, I had signs of the cancer when I found two lumps in my right breast. However, after an ultrasound and mammogram the doctors ruled them out from being cancerous. Then, in 2009 I discovered that they were growing. Also, I had a large lump under my armpit that caused me great concern. After considering what to do about it, I decided to wait to see if it went away. So, one day, I was in the tub singing praises to the Lord. My entire body became extremely hot and I felt as if it was going to explode. When I reached under my arm to wash, the lump was gone. Immediately, I jumped out of the tub, wrapped myself in a towel and called the children, Patrick and Candace. I showed them the difference under each arm. The children, two witnesses, acknowledged that there was extra skin under my right arm. Blessed God my Savior!

The lump under my arm miraculously vanished, but I don't know why God didn't heal the ones in my breast. What I do know is that God had other plans and showed me that parabens and excess sugar were not for me. In fact, once I rid myself of parabens found in lotion, make-up and hair products, the more noticeable lump in my breast started to decrease in size. Having changed my routine, God showed me the continued benefit of a healthy lifestyle to eat lots of fresh fruits and vegetables, and His cleansing power.

During my treatment I had a wonderful breast surgeon and a terrible disease. My tumor was so hard that during the second biopsy, it bent the needle. However, Dr. Deborah Norris was determined to get the correct diagnosis and helped me on my path to good health. She even checked on the care I received from my other physicians. God bless her for the superior care she provided.

Not only did God send a great surgeon, He also allowed me to reconnect with my sister and grow closer to my older and younger brothers. How ironic, this sickness that caused me great loss and pain, was instrumental in strengthening and mending relationships. Since our parents were gone, Mom wasn't there to keep the heart of our family beating and Dad, the rock, was no longer there to motivate our successes. Mom the matrix couldn't reach from Heaven and fix us anymore. Regardless of our differences, God saw fit to bless me with a good family who loved me. He gave me the opportunity to live and to be a mother to my children Candace and Patrick, to cherish Elshaad, like a son, and to be an Aunt to Kris, Zakiya, Madeline, and Zack.

The cancer treatment left me with pneumonitis, neuropathy, lymphedema, fatigue and hearing loss in my right ear. A TIA or Transient Ischemic Attack/mini stroke caused vision loss in my left eye. I later suffered another. Thank God my hearing and sight were restored. Despite the fatigue, weight gain and great efforts to focus, I was still blessed.

In the past, I had been very sick few times. Cancer struck at the least likely time. Being under fifty and very healthy, I was resigned to eat the dietary clean foods of the Bible. Without any sickness, outside of a sinus infection, brought on by disobedience, I remained absolutely healthy for sixteen years.

When I was a young child I had the chicken pox, and the measles simultaneously. Also, around the age of fourteen, I lived in Tanzania and may have contracted malaria. There was never a medical diagnosis, but my fever and chills, treated at the infirmary, were characteristic of the disease. As aforementioned, I had cancer. Also, having the flu once, I prayed to never have it again, so far so good. My last three bouts with serious sinus infections have ended, as well.

During the time that I had both the chicken pox and measles my temperature was uncontrollable and I was hospitalized. Made to sleep on a hard, cooling bed, I was absolutely miserable. My discomfort was unbearable and my mother had to leave to go home. In my distress, I called out incessantly for her. Unable to quiet me, the nurses left me alone.

At a point of complete despair I saw a person, I thought was a nurse, enter my room. She told me it was going to be all right and stroked my arm. Expecting her to soon tire of me and leave, she kept comforting me. When I quieted she got up and left.

A few minutes later, my nurse came in the room. I told her that the other nurse was so nice. She said, " Little girl no one has been in your room, I'm…" and stopped. I said, " She went out over there." When I opened my eyes wide enough to see the entire room, I saw that I was pointing at the wall. My nurse looked frightened and backed out of the room. She refused to enter my room for the rest of the night, but made an appearance at the door with others.

God had sent an angel to minister to me in my distress. I had seen my angel for the first time. She had blonde hair that was styled in a braid that wrapped around her head. I never forgot how she helped me and refused to leave me until I was comforted. This speaks to the patience of God and His loving kindness.

Having overcome devastating illnesses, I continue to eat the healthy Jewish diet of the Bible. Though I don't keep all of the specific eating protocols and dietary restrictions, I avoid the foods that God deems unclean: shellfish, fish without scales, pork and other restricted animals. Also, I refrain from eating the blood in the flesh, (Leviticus 17:10-14); fish without scales, often have parasites; the shellfish clean toxins out of the water; and pork has adverse effects.

Following the diet similar to Christ's, a practicing Jew, helped me to have a strong immune system. How I got cancer, I don't know. The doctors were all surprised to see how well I was able to withstand the treatment. Well, I told them God helped me, or I ate by Deuteronomy. Sometimes, I just said I've been healthy most of my life.

The scripture referencing the eating of meat used the word broma. Here is a reference for broma:

http://www.bibletools.org/index.cfm/fuseaction/Lexicon.show/ID/G1033/broma.htm

Strong's #1033: broma (pronounced bro'-mah) from the base of 977; food (literally or figuratively), especially (ceremonially) articles allowed or forbidden by the Jewish law:--meat, victuals.

Thayer's Greek Lexicon:
brōma
1) that which is eaten, food
Part of Speech: noun neuter
Relation: from the base of G977

FAITH

Citing in TDNT: 1:642, 111
Usage: This word is used 17 times:

Matthew 14:15: "the villages, they may buy to themselves food."
Mark 7:19: "drain it doth go out, purifying all the meats"
Luke 3:11: "none, and he having victuals."
Luke 9:13: "we may buy for all this people victuals."
John 4:34: "Jesus said to them, 'My food is, that I may do the will of Him who sent me, and may finish His work...'"
Romans 14:15: "and if through victuals thy brother is grieved, no more dost thou walk according to love."
Romans 14:15: "do not with thy victuals destroy that one for whom Christ died"
Romans 14:20: "for the sake of victuals cast not down the work of God"
1 Corinthians 3:2: "with milk I fed you, and not with meat, for ye were not yet able, but not even yet are ye now able,"
1 Corinthians 6:13: " Meats [are] for the belly"
1 Corinthians 6:13: "and the belly for the meats "
1 Corinthians 8:8: "But victuals do not commend us not to God"
1 Corinthians 8:13: "Wherefore, if victuals cause my brother to stumble, I may eat no"
1 Corinthians 10:2-3: "and all to Moses were baptized in the cloud, and in the sea; and all the same spiritual food did eat"
1 Timothy 4:3: "forbidding to marry – abstain from meats that God created to be received"
Hebrews 9:10: " only in victuals and drinks, and different baptisms,"
Hebrews 13:9: "good that by grace the heart be confirmed, not with meats, in which they who were occupied were not profited"

Dietary constraints have brought about many conflicts in the Church. Here, I have included personal benefits from eating the foods deemed clean in the Bible. These decisions must be made with the goal in mind to follow Christ and the leading of the Holy Spirit. My leading, from the Spirit of God, resulted in a healthier, stronger body. Each believer has to abstain from foods per God's command for her or him.

Personally, God repeatedly showed me Isaiah 66:17, Leviticus 11 and Deuteronomy 14. So, I know God wants me to restrict my diet. Although I also avoid shellfish and shrimp, I have no problem eating meats that are not certified as kosher. We avoid eating hidden pork products made with gelatin from pig's skin, which are found in many popular brands of marshmallows, along with most gummy vitamins and fruit snacks.

The food additive L-Cysteine or E920, in our favorite bagels, bread and other food originates from human hair. Synthetic forms, along with duck feathers and other materials are in use, as well. As a result, we refrain from eating foods with this ingredient listed on the packaging. Be aware that some kosher items do contain this ingredient. If the food label lists a dough conditioner, this may be L-Cysteine. Visit the web site below, for an extensive, but incomplete listing of clean and unclean food products:

http://www.theisraelofgodrc.com/CUPL.html

Also, for information about L-Cysteine and other food additives visit:
http://www.laleva.cc/food/enumbers/E901-970.html

During Peter's ministry food restrictions were a matter of contention, as they are now. Although Peter was commissioned by God to evangelize the circumcision (Galatians 2:8), he ate with the uncircumcised, and then abandoned them when James and other Jews visited. This behavior brought a severe reprimand from Paul. Not only had Peter compromised the teaching of oneness in Christ, he led others, like Barnabas, to alienate the uncircumcised (Galatians 2:13). Had Peter continued on a path of unrighteousness, as a believer, he was in jeopardy of corrupting the message of salvation offered through Christ. Paul considered this an attempt to ensure righteousness by following the law, which was antithetical to the righteousness found in Christ.

God subsequently wanted Peter to expand his ministry beyond the Jewish people to the nations. So, in a dream, God showed Peter unclean animals and told him to, "kill and eat" (Acts 10:13). God signified to Peter that fellowship with non-Jews was His will. God wanted Peter to do something unthinkable and fellowship with non-Jews. Uniting Jewish and non-Jewish believers was the objective, not eating the unclean food.

So, what relation does that have to diet? Consuming clean or unclean meats has no bearing on salvation with Christ. We do have the choice to eat whatever we want, but there are better, healthier ways to eat. Taking the cues from the Bible is my preferred method. By avoiding pork, shellfish, other unclean meat, bottled water, plastics, meats with steroids, pesticides, and genetically modified or altered foods, I protect my body and strengthen my immune system. Now, more than ever, I persevere to maintain good health. In fact, I find that juicing is necessary to keep my body healthy. Normally, I drink fresh squeezed lemonade and limeade sweetened with maple syrup, raw sugar or without any sweeteners. At times, I use the blender to liquefy the fruits and vegetables into a smoothie, rather than using the juicer. This also makes cleaning up easier.

Household pesticides may also have played a role in my development of breast cancer. I avoid using pesticides, especially feminizing types, due to high concentrations of estrogen. I also use cleaners that are non-toxic or wear gloves when handling harsh chemicals.

While on chemotherapy, I drank about 5 to 6 bottles of water daily. I was encouraged to stay hydrated and now know that cancer dislikes an alkaline environment. Even after a complete regimen of adriamycin and cytoxan, plus all, but the final treatment of taxotere, my tumor was still 7cm. Apparently the two lumps had merged. Unfortunately, plastic in the body mimics estrogen called xenoestrogen and latches onto the cell, like a puzzle piece, similar to estrogen. Estrogen and progesterone trigger the cancer growth in breast cancers with ER/PR receptors. Having breast cancer with estrogen and progesterone receptors, the plastic found in the bottles was perhaps a contributor to the growth of my tumor. So, now, I don't drink water from plastic bottles. Even if the bottle is kept cool, the plastic may have already leached into the contents during transport. For that reason, I stopped drinking bottled water, but began to drink filtered water, instead. I certainly had no intention to give my cells any fuel to become cancerous.

These endocrine disruptors may be investigated online. One credible source was found at the National Center for Biotechnology Information: http://www.ncbi.nlm.nih.gov/pubmed/19274472

Continuing on, the author of the book of Hebrews defines faith: "And faith is of things hoped for a confidence, of matters not seen a conviction" (Hebrews 11:1). God gives a spirit to each of us, in order to download His content. Our spirits allow us to communicate with

God, even before becoming a believer and provide each person with a unique ability to recognize the things of God. When a person accepts the salvation Christ offers, God gives faith as an assurance for the believer to then, trust God and hope in Him to perform what cannot be seen. (See http://biblehub.com/greek/5287.htm)

Receiving the portion or "measure of faith" (Romans 12:3) allows the believer to hope in things unseen that are provable and evident. Seeing that faith comes from God, it is safe to say that only God is able to convince us to believe in Him, but we must chose to follow. Even knowing the truth, we still may reject the knowledge. We have a choice with God to receive His gift of faith through His active works.

Lovingly, God extended His grace and mercy to those who died before Christ's ministry on the earth. Jesus had always been a part of God: Father, Son and Spirit. Although the three entities acted independently, only one Spirit possessed one nature and one desire existed. Since everything was created through Jesus (John 1:1-3; Colossians 1:16), every believer has lived with "a measure of faith" (Romans 12:3) and the persuasion of God expectantly. Faith from God has given believers hope. The evidence of that faith was the manifestation of the unseen. Their "measure of faith" given to believers by God only and manifested in their relationship with the Father caused them to believe and to trust God. Jesus the Messiah said to the Pharisees, " 'If me ye had known, my Father also ye had known' " (John 8:19). To those who believed in Jesus he said to the Jews who believed in Him, " 'If ye may remain in my word, truly my disciples ye are, and ye shall know the truth, and the truth shall make you free' " (John 8:31-32).

There is no Biblical reference of souls waiting in limbo for Christ to deliver them, now. However, the souls waiting for their bodies to be raised from the dead are to be judged for their works (Revelation 20:12). Remember Jesus said, "…My sheep hear my voice…" (John 10:27). Those not found written in the scroll of life (Revelation 20:15) will be cast into the lake of the fire with the devil, the false prophet and the beast (Revelation 20: 13-14).

Our likeness to God codifies the essential difference between humans and other created beings. Unlike animals, people have God's resemblance in the physical and spiritual forms. As mentioned in Isaiah

31:3, the horse is flesh, but not spirit. Job tells us that God gives life to all living things and spirit to mankind (Job 12:10). Also, Acts 2:17-18 mentions God pouring His Spirit on all flesh resulting in people seeing dreams and prophesying. Since animals do not have spirits, their intellectual ability facilitates communication. The human spirit exceeds this limitation. It is important to point out that even though Balaam's donkey sees the angel with the flaming sword, God allows the donkey to utter words in response to the cruelty of Balaam and fearing responds in the flesh to protect her master (Numbers 22:28).

When contemplating spiritual matters, one filters this information through the soul. Every soul (personality and mind) is individual to each person. Even when sharing similar beliefs, the measure of faith that God places in each of us (Romans 12:3), affords a person with the opportunity to choose to believe in Him. By responding to God and accepting His Word, individuals have the capacity to answer the call of God. Thus maturing in spiritual matters and leaving carnal desires behind brings life and peace to the mind (Romans 8:1-6). Consequently, doing the work of God illuminates that the Spirit leads the believer (Romans 8:14-15).

Our souls have the intellect to engage spiritually and to make eternal choices. Also, the soul asks the questions and ponders. Although the soul initiates these interactions with God on a spiritual level, it is the spirit acting apart from the soul that engages God responding first to God's call in a direct line of communication. Our souls, spirits and bodies witness the encounter(s) of the other(s) and fuel belief. Faith, apart from belief, is present in every believer. For someone who is unable to access teaching about God, God personally and through His creation communicates directly with an individual. Also, because the body houses the soul and the spirit, spiritual expressions may cause physical manifestations to occur. These evidences may be Godly, such as Moses glowing after speaking with God (Exodus 34:35); or demonic, as the demoniacs of the Gergesenes region (Matthew 8:28), the Gadarenes (Mark 5:1-6; Luke 8:26, 27, 29).

God is of the living, " 'And concerning the rising again of the dead, did ye not read that which was spoken to you by God, saying, 'I am the God of Abraham, and the God of Isaac, and the God of Jacob? God is not a God of dead men, but of living' " (Matthew 22:31-32). As the

Bible describes the lives of God's servants: Abraham, Isaac and Jacob. Jesus' example also shows us the importance of knowing and obeying the Father. If we belong to God, we obey Him, as well, and keep the life of our souls and spirits. By obeying God, rather than our desires, we love God more.

Through redemption spiritual descendants of Abraham inherit all the blessings of God. Having Abraham's bloodline is just that. One must also have a spiritual connection of salvation. This means the Spirit leads God's children. All who have salvation, through the Messiah, Jesus Christ, by-pass the judgment of the second death, the lake of fire. So, with Christ sitting at the right hand of the Father, He also keeps the sheep to His right. " The affirmation of Jehovah to my Lord: 'Sit at My right hand, Till I make thine enemies thy footstool' " (Psalm 110:1 and Matthew 22:44).

The goats are to Christ's left and go to the Father for punishment. "Then shall he say also to those on the left hand, Go ye from me, the cursed, to the fire, the age-during, that hath been prepared for the Devil and his messengers: for I did hunger, and ye gave me not to eat; I did thirst and ye gave me not to drink; a stranger I was, and ye did not receive me; naked, and ye put not around me; infirm, and in prison, and ye did not look after me. 'Then shall they answer, they also, saying, Lord, when did we see thee hungering, or thirsting, or a stranger, or naked, or infirm, or in prison, and we did not minister to thee? 'Then shall he answer them, saying, Verily I say to you, Inasmuch as ye did [it] not to one of these, the least, ye did [it] not to me. And these shall go away to punishment age-during, but the righteous to life age-during' " (Matthew 25:41-46).

While we are alive, our spirits have the liberty to talk with God. Without Christ, at death, the spirit becomes trapped with the soul separated from God. Neither is free to dialogue with God. This means the soul has lost the opportunity to petition God. Eventually, people hearing the final judgment for their deeds are cast into darkness. Sin outweighs all of their good deeds rendering them worthless. Souls, without the forgiveness of sin, which Jesus offers freely and without reservation, for eternity are subject to confinement in Hades, and then the second death (Revelation 20:14). Avoiding this end should cause one to desire the protection Christ offers. How awful it is for a spirit that has unbridled communication with God, to be subject to torment unable to engage Him, and never again have the opportunity to experience His peace or His forgiveness.

Paul depicts God's steadfastness by describing how nothing is able to separate anyone from His love (Romans 8). This assurance in God reveals a foundation for all believers to build upon. As we hold onto the mercy of God, His promise to cleanse us should resound in the hearts of believers. With God abiding in the believer, there exists the desire to live out his/her calling and to be whole spiritually. Paul considers the work of God and His commitment to believers. "God of the peace Himself sanctify you wholly and may your whole spirit, and soul, and body, be preserved unblameably in the presence of our Lord Jesus Christ; steadfast Is He who is calling you, who also will do [it]" (I Thessalonians 5:23).

Before Jesus was crucified, He was confident that Satan had been defeated. "Now is a judgment of this world, now shall the ruler of this world be cast forth..." (John 12:31). Also, we saw His conviction in John 16:11, "and concerning judgment, because the ruler of this world hath been judged." When God pronounced His judgment, in John Chapter 12, the people heard thunder and others said, " 'a Messenger hath spoken to him' " (John 12:29). The people were witnesses to the acknowledgement of the Son by the Father. One could say, God positively charged the negative atmosphere. Thus revealing the conscience of God to always know what is good and work to perform it.

Christ's victory over Satan gives believers the power to exercise their senses to discern good from evil (Hebrews 5:14). Rebuffing the evil of unbelief, believers only enter into Christ's rest by hearing the Word of God, and God combines His Word with faith (Hebrews 3:19; 4:2; 4:6). Through a process God matures believers to understand the Word (Hebrew 4:2; 5:8-14). Therefore, I posit that confidence in God is an outcome of the faith that Christ places in every believer to serve in her or his individual capacities (Romans 12:3-8). It is only through God's strength that believers are able to accomplish this: "For all things I have strength, in Christ's strengthening me" (Philippians 4:13). The strength is from Christ and the evidence of His joy is in believers. As we endeavor to live holy, let us daily give God our burdens and elicit

His angels to minister to us (Psalm 91:11; Hebrews 1:14). Since Christ fought and won the battle on the cross, He is certainly able to solve our problems.

Apostle Paul faced opposition from within and without. To gain victory over the flesh was a struggle very familiar to him. Although ship wrecked, beaten with rods and left for dead many times (II Corinthians 11:23, 25; Acts 14:19), Paul promoted the things of God over his own concerns (Colossians 1:24-29). Repeatedly abused and imprisoned for his conviction, Paul remained committed to walking with Jesus. Pressing forward to die to the flesh, Paul fought well. Evidenced in his personal conversion and passion to encourage others in the Lord, he strove in his faith and remained steadfast (I Timothy 6:12).

In Revelation, Christ embraced believers at their deaths. Those who had faith in the beast, who bowed to him or his image or took the mark of the beast received God's wrath. Consequently, Christ rejected those who embraced the beast, because they had chosen to reject Him. John described the faith of both believers and unbelievers to reveal the depth of faith necessary to overcome evil. He also illuminated the saints' endurance to follow God, "keeping the commandments of God and the faith of Jesus" (Revelation 14:12).

There were 144,000 Jewish men who would come from the twelve tribes of Israel as God's first fruits, protected to fulfill His purpose on the earth with God's name written on their foreheads (Revelation 4:8; 14:1, 4). These men, as the other saints, refused to bow to the beast, his image or to take the mark of the beast. Also, they were virgins who had not defiled themselves with women (Revelation 14:4). Studying the scripture showed that men were physically defiled by their semen, after sex with women, through seminal emissions (Leviticus 15:32) and ejaculation (Deuteronomy 23:10). Although seminal emissions defiled men, this verse included women; therefore, the defilement avoided seemed to be in keeping with Deuteronomy 23:10 and this led to my conclusion that the 144,000 were men. This also explained why the priest wanted David's guarantee that the men would not be with women prior to eating the bread from the temple. Their seminal emissions caused defilement.

Clearing the way for all to overcome the power of evil, John revealed the path to follow: to walk circumspectly with God and judge with righteous judgment (John 7:24). The judgment of the world and of its ruler occurred when God glorified His name and was to glorify it again (John 12:28). As a result judgment fell on the false god of this world. Once ejected from Heaven, Satan had been cast forth or out for us to see him, accursed (Isaiah 14:12-17).

Satan's downfall came when he executed an ill-fated plan to overthrow God. Foolishly he wanted to be as powerful as God and believed it was possible (Isaiah 14:14). Considering and acknowledging God's sovereignty was unacceptable to Satan. In my opinion, this refusal to see God as the All Mighty by committing to self-reliance has been the chief hindrance to salvation. Generally, focused primarily on self-promotion, personal endeavors, accolades, prizes and reputations resulted in fame and fortune for many. However, great and necessary those accomplishments may have been, trusting in a meaningful relationship with God has proven to be the nexus that linked souls to our Creator.

So, rather than relying on what the world has to offer, one should seek more precious treasure with eternal value. In pursuit of a higher calling, God gives us the tools to ensure our success. As Paul instructs, "put on the whole armor of God, for your being able to stand against the wiles of the devil" (Ephesians 6:11). When believers put on the whole armor of God, we have the ability to defend ourselves from spiritual attacks and possess the authority to direct, to encourage and to help others. United believers must use this alliance to support the body of Christ.

The first epistle of John, eloquently described the work of believers as acts in both deed and truth. In I John 3:17-18 he wrote, "and whoever may have the goods of the world, and may view his brother having need, and may shut up his bowels from him – how doth the love of God remain in him? My little children, may we not love in word nor in tongue, but in word and in truth! " Also, as believers, John teaches us to know that if our hearts condemn us, God has the power to condemn us all the more. It is with boldness and a heart free from condemnation that one approaches God to receive what he or she asks of Him.

When someone keeps God's commands He abides in him or her and that person correspondingly abides in Him. The Spirit gives evidence to a believer. John outlines the significance of these concepts. He also details the importance of following God's command, specifically by loving one another, to please God. He iterates, "and in this we know that of the truth we are, and before Him we shall assure our hearts, because if our heart may condemn – because greater is God than our heart, and He doth know all things. Beloved, if our heart may not condemn us, we have boldness toward God, and whatever we may ask, we receive from Him because His commands we keep, and the things pleasing before Him we do, and this is His command, that we may believe in the name of His Son Jesus Christ, and may love one another, even as He did give command to us, and he who is keeping His commands, in Him he doth remain, and He in him; and in this we know that He doth remain in us, from the Spirit that He gave us" (I John 3:19-24).

The works bring faith to life, and works also perfect faith. In James chapter two, verse 22, faith integrates with works producing a perfected faith: "dost thou see that the faith was working with his works, and out of the works the faith was perfected? and fulfilled was the Writing that is saying, 'And Abraham did believe God, and it was reckoned to him -- to righteousness;' and, 'Friend of God' he was called. Ye see, then, that out of works is man declared righteous, and not out of faith only; and in like manner also Rahab the harlot -- was she not out of works declared righteous, having received the messengers, and by another way having sent forth? for as the body apart from the spirit is dead, so also the faith apart from the works is dead" (James 2:22-26). (Genesis 22:9 has the account of Abraham offering Isaac as a sacrifice on the altar; Rahab's works of righteousness may be found in Joshua 2).

So, if faith without works is dead (James 2:17), then combining works with faith brings faith to life. Thus God combines faith with His works to judge. Faith comes from God, so for a believer to be righteous he or she must perform actions suitable to God. Righteousness is separate from salvation, which is a free gift. The work of obeying God's command, particularly obeying God's command to love one another and to keep His commands shows God residing in the believer. John depicts an active believer who works to obey God and to abide in Him.

By abiding in God, through an activated faith, the believer manifests the righteousness of God.

Consequently, John tells the believer to have boldness and not to be ashamed before God in His presence (I John 2:27-29). Since God has a greater power than the condemnation of our hearts, we must live to please God without shame. By loving one another and keeping His commands, we are able to confidently stand before God making our petitions and receiving them. Thus those requests from a heart with the Spirit of God may be free from condemnation.

This signifies the submission of the believer to God, showing humility, faith, and boldness, all in effect. Hence the believer, who ministers in love to benefit others, shows the Spirit of God is dwelling in him or her. For example, God blesses Solomon with such great wisdom and wealth, because of his desire to judge and to serve the people in his charge (II Chronicles 1:11-13; I Kings 3:6-14).

So, having established that works produced a perfected faith, let us turn our attention to Jesus. In John 6:29, Jesus said the work of God was to believe in Him whom God sent. Speaking about Himself in the Spirit, Jesus wanted believers to eat his flesh and drink his blood. This was the flesh and blood of God or the Word. Our flesh benefited nothing; the goal was and presently to eradicate spiritual hunger and thirst (John 6:63). Being the Messiah, Jesus knew it was necessary for us to feed the soul and spirit by consuming Him or the Word. Therefore, reading and studying the Bible has been the single most essential key to the development of a believer and the reception of faith.

Prosperity of the soul and spirit was the lesson Christ taught. As our Salvation, Christ offered Himself as a means to generate spiritual wealth. Hosea 10:12 and James 3:18 showed how believers found prosperity by believing, sowing righteousness, reaping kindness and peace. At times, material wealth and riches were evidence of righteousness in the Bible. However, Deuteronomy 28 records examples of wealth reserved as blessings from God.

God promises to bless Israel with abundance of goods, children, herds, and land, subsequent to following His commandments. Today, believers continue to follow God's commandments by the law of the

Spirit (Romans 8:2; Galatians 3:1-5), as seen in their fruit. With Christ abiding in a believer, one has the fruit of the Spirit. This manifestation reveals if that individual genuinely follows Christ. Galatians 5:22-23, lists the fruit: "And the fruit of the Spirit is: Love, joy, peace, long-suffering, kindness, goodness, faith, meekness, temperance".

Luke 8:1-15 revealed the way to prosperity. To hear and to retain the Word of God, or seed, resulted in 'an hundred fold' production of fruit continually. When the word was not believed unto salvation, Satan came and took the word out of the heart. Also, there were those who with joy heard, received the word, and believed over a period of time, but without any root, fell away for temptation. Another group had seed that fell on the thorns. They believed, but experienced incomplete prosperity. This group heard the word, but submitted to "…anxieties, and riches, and pleasures of life, and choked, and bear not to completion" (Luke 8:13-14). The word that fell on good ground represented those who "in an upright and good heart, having heard the word, do retain [it], and bear fruit in continuance" (Luke 8:15).

God's command was conveyed in Peter's writing "… brethren, be diligent to make stedfast your calling and choice, for these things doing, ye may never stumble, for so, richly shall be superadded to you the entrance into the age-during reign of our Lord and Saviour Jesus Christ" (II Peter 1:10-11). Simon Peter, an apostle of Jesus Christ, afforded believers with the way to achieve a fruitful return. Acknowledgment of God and escape from the corruption of this world's desires, Peter conceded that this gave the ability to be fruitful, abounding in a purpose directed by God. He says, "…superadd in your faith the worthiness, and in the worthiness the knowledge, and in the knowledge the temperance, and in the temperance the endurance, and in the endurance the piety, and in the piety the brotherly kindness, and in the brotherly kindness the love" (II Peter 1: 5-8). To be mindful to exhibit the right temperament, simultaneously with endurance in all circumstances to serve God and to be holy, to treat others as brothers, encapsulated the picture of a believer and Christian, Peter described.

Indeed this is a high calling and choice for a believer to maintain, but essential for sowing to the Spirit. With God's help alone are believers able to surmount this task. Having the intellect, desire and will to serve God comes only from surrendering to the fact that we are incapable of being gods ourselves. Made in the image of God, we have the capacity to make choices and defy the odds, but, if we are not translated, eventually succumb to death. Let that death be physical and not eternal. Living for God means submitting to Him and in that submission comes true freedom from God's Spirit (II Corinthians 3:17). Knowing who you are in Christ eliminates doubt of purpose and fear of being overcome by failure. The scripture, Proverbs 24:16, tells us even though the righteous falls he or she rises again. " For seven [times] doth the righteous fall and rise …" When we make mistakes, we know that God will help us up to try again. Anyone who exhibits God's love offers the same help.

Transitioning to David's younger days as a shepherd, he tended and protected his flock with his life. Fearlessly, David faced a lion and a bear. Therefore, a man was no match for him. He knew God was able to protect him from an "uncircumcised Philistine". In fact, David confidently entered the battle to win against the enemy of God. After all the conquests God gave David, why did he sin? One may simply surmise, but he did overcome to please God.

To the people of Judah and Israel God commanded: "innocent blood do not shed in this place" (Jeremiah 7:6). Those decisions rested on God. God made the choice to take the life of David and Bathsheba's son. Also, after David numbered the troops, God sent the angel to kill the people. Of the choices David had, he chose to be in God's hand, rather than his enemies. Taking responsibility for his actions, David showed his humility to admit his fault, and faith from God to know Israel would survive.

Truly our faith must have works in order to come alive. God works in us to finish the faith He gives. Loving God is doing His will. This action is righteousness. God's first and greatest commandment is to love Him with all your heart, soul and mind; and second, love your neighbor as yourself (Matthew 22:36-40). We must set our minds to know, if God wants something to happen, it will. The work is God's and He combines faith with work. God's work perfects faith. Operating under that premise sets the foundation of trust and belief.

Knowing people were unable to hinder God's will, the Pharisee, Gameliel, alluded to man's inability to stop the work of God. In Acts

5:34-42, Gameliel told the Sanhedrim, if the disciples of Jesus were of God, they could not stop them. Jesus also spoke of the work of God and to believe in Him whom God sent (John 6:29). Also, to call on His name or His authority and to appeal to God saved or rescued from the penalty of sin and its power (Acts 2:21; Romans 10:13; Strong's Concordance 4982).

Last, God commands His children to be holy, because He is holy (Leviticus 11:44-45; 19:2; 20:7, 26; 21:8; I Peter 1:16). God saves us for a holy calling, not to our works, but His (II Timothy 1:9). We must refrain from fornication or sex outside of a married husband and wife. Sexual sin causes untold heartache, disease and destruction of the soul and the spirit. With conviction, "stand against the Devil and he will flee from you" (James 4:7). Keep telling yourself and others, "No, I will not sin against God." Be holy, cleanout the filth that tempts you and remove yourself from unhealthy situations. By keeping your eyes on God, and seeking His Kingdom, you will have contentment to serve God and give Him glory. Trust in the faith He places in you and perfects.

Faith of the believer overcomes the world. Believers know Jesus is the Son of God who is come through water and blood as the Spirit testifies in the earth with the Father and the Son (I John 5:4-8).

Applications for the Five Characteristics
&
Additional Information

Campaigns

Complaining was a problem for us in our family. For the purposes of this book, complaining is a lack of faith hindering believers from experiencing the fullness of God. Setting parameters for complaining, for this context, include: expressing a feeling of discontentment when things are not going our way, and dragging others down with negative comments, rather than building up and edifying. Carrying a weight of discontentment results in letting others know of this unhappiness without Godly resolve.

For about four summers, my daughter and I went on 'God campaigns'. That is to say, we found one item of contention to overcome. Well, generally I would seek the Lord for a topic. When He revealed one to me, I would tell Candace, my daughter. One year, God showed us that we needed to stop complaining. So, of course, that became our campaign. These campaigns generally began and ended each summer. For weeks we reminded each other not to complain. When traffic was unbearable, as usual, I would complain. Candace would remind me not to complain. I, of course, would point out the need to complain, and she would remind me not to complain. When the reminders diminished we ended the campaign.

To elaborate: When in traffic, instead of saying, " Why doesn't that person move?" My daughter would say, "Mom, you're not complaining are you?" I would then say snidely, "Maybe they need prayer". My daughter would say, "Mom...", and I would agree, apologetically, that perhaps God was keeping us from having an accident.

Jesus said he did the will of His Father (John 6:38). How do believers come to the realization that God is in control, without being afraid of circumstances? Well, the answer is simple, but perhaps hard to accept. Let God be God and just be. If one adopts the principle of Paul to be abased and to abound (Philippians 4:12), the peace of God will remain. Paul and Silas sang praises to God in prison, because of their contentment. David sang praises to God and blessed the Lord, at all times (Psalm 34:1).

Why would slow traffic cause one to give up hope? It's time to stop looking at the immediate, reach out and help someone else. Help with gladness in our hearts not showing how good we are, but to honor Christ's love by giving to our neighbors. Believers need to remember working for God means believing in Jesus, the bread of God, true bread, bread of the life, living bread (Matthew 6:29, 32, 33, 48, 51). Thus refraining from vain work, but following the holy calling of God. By giving God the glory, we have the strength to complete His work and the motivation to encourage others (Psalm 115). Paul called it "...the good strife of faith" (I Timothy 6:12).

Our complaining acts as an opening for Satan to hinder believers from accomplishing God's work. Our fight is spiritual, so believers must put on the whole armor of God and pray continually (Ephesians 6:10-13; I Thessalonians 5:17).

Defeating the Enemies

As a child, I used to watch boxing with my dad. How my dad loved the sport. Spending time with him was great fun, but I couldn't watch the match for long. Regrettably, I left the comfort of my dad's side, because the brutality of boxing was too intense. However, just like a prizefighter determined to knockout the contender, we must be committed to beat Satan's brains in or out.

Once, I had a strange dream that I was walking along a road and some thing was threatening me. Attempting to avoid a conflict, I kept walking. When I looked back there were more of them. Soon, I realized that I had to confront them or risk severe injury. Seeking shelter I entered the nearest building. I noticed that it was empty. The walls, steps, floor and ceiling were all made of marble. Realizing the enemies had followed me I turned to engage them. They began to fly around the room. I said, I can do that too and proceeded to fly through the air. As these beings lunged at me, I grabbed them and tossed them to the floor. With great effort, I smashed them and punished them, but they kept rebounding. Finally, I became too exhausted to continue. When the enemies were about to overtake me, I forced myself to wake from the dream.

When I awoke, I asked God why I could not defeat the enemies. He told me that I hadn't called the angels. So, the next time I had that dream, I prayed for the angels to fight for me. Faithfully, God sent the angels to fight. This time, when the angels threw my enemies to the floor, they didn't recover. They just lay smashed on the floor!

God gives believers powerful resources to defeat the enemy. As I know to call and to access my help, other believers need this information, as well. Through God's authority, He shows me how to request the help of angels. They are quick to respond to fight for my protection. Believers must pray for complete victory over Satan and his demons, forever. With a hedge of protection around me, God keeps the enemies at bay. God offers this safety to all.

DEFEATING THE ENEMIES

In Acts 26:6 Paul made his plea before King Agrippa. He presented his case against his confinement for preaching the hope of God's promise, Jesus. Again in Rome, Acts 28:17-20, key Jewish men of the community gathered. Paul, in chains, appealed to the men for the hope of Israel. Having started on the wrong path, he persecuted many Jewish believers in the past. Now, Paul passionately and lovingly revealed Christ to fellow Jews and others. As a believer, he encouraged all to turn to God. The author told the reader in Acts 26:18, 20, "…to open their eyes, to turn [them] from darkness to light, and [from] the authority of the Adversary unto God, for their receiving forgiveness of sins, and a lot among those having been sanctified, by faith that [is] toward me." Also, he said, "…but to those in Damascus first, and to those in Jerusalem, to all the region also of Judea, and to the nations, I was preaching to reform, and to turn back unto God, doing works worthy of reformation."

Flawed as David was, he had faith, Godly contentment and believed in the Lord's promise of a Messiah. David wrote, "the affirmation of Jehovah to my Lord: 'Sit at My right hand, Till I make thine enemies thy footstool' " (Psalm 110:1). Also, David had a prophetic anointing. " '…And lo thou [art] to them as a singer of doting loves, A pleasant voice, and playing well on an instrument, And they have heard thy words, and they are not doing them. And in its coming in -- lo, it hath come, And they have known that a prophet hath been in their midst!' " (Ezekiel 33:32-33).

As believers we have trusted in our Lord and Savior, Jesus Christ. Christ came and died for our spiritual cleansing. "And he is pierced for our transgressions, Bruised for our iniquities, The chastisement of our peace [is] on him, And by his bruise there is healing to us" (Isaiah 53:5). God made Him who was without sin, sin for us (II Corinthians 5:21). God has given Himself to cleanse us, " 'Lo, the Lamb of God, who is taking away the sin of the world…' " (John 1:29).

This eternal hope that we have in Christ is our only Salvation and way to remove sin (Hebrews 9:26). While the Law bound David and those under the Old Covenant, God still chose to give the Jews a new covenant. "For this [is] the covenant that I make, With the house of Israel, after those days, An affirmation of Jehovah, I have given My law in their inward part, And on their heart I do write it, And I have been to them for God, And they are to me for a people" (Jeremiah 31:33). Solomon wrote in Proverbs 3:1, "My son! My law forget not, And my commandments let thy heart keep."

Similar verses in Hebrews 8:10 and 10:16 give all believers the promise of God's word to be written on our hearts and minds. Jesus Christ tore the veil releasing the Spirit of God to unite gender, ethnicity, nationality, and color into one new race of people working together as one body, the Church. This is done when the Father draws us to the Son (John 6:44). Once we receive salvation, at death we are able to stand before the Father, because no one comes to the Father except by the Son (John 14:6). When we die or are translated, we are able to stand before the Father, without fear of destruction from His wrath. I may personally attest, through my testimony, that the Father does draw us to His Son. This work of God epitomizes the perfection of faith. In James 2:22-26 faith plus works equals the perfection of faith, "dost thou see that the faith was working with his works, and out of the works the faith was perfected?"

Years ago, as I was reading God's word, God revealed to me that Caiaphas, the high priest, knew that Jesus was the Messiah (John 11:49-52, "…Caiaphas being chief priest of that year, said to them, 'Ye have not known anything, nor reason that it is good for us that one man may die for the people, and not the whole nation perish. And this he said not of himself, but being chief priest of that year, he did prophesy that Jesus was about to die for the nation, and not for the nation only, but that also the children of God, who have been scattered abroad, he may gather together into one." Teaching, Jesus said the authorities knew who He was (John 7:28). Also, John 18:14, "and Caiaphas was he who gave counsel to the Jews, that it is good for one man to perish for the people." This time, it was one life for all lives, the fulfillment of the Law. No longer were the sacrifices of animals necessary, nor could they remove sin (Hebrews 10:11). The shed blood of Jesus Christ was made available to wipe away sin completely. Christ, The Anointed One, Messiah, Yeshua, Lamb of God was the only one worthy to finalize God's Covenant.

Remember God said, "…. my life I lay down for the sheep" (John 10:15). Jesus became a man to be the sacrifice for sin and to fulfill the role of the chief-priest: "wherefore it did behove him in all things to be made like to the brethren, that he might become a kind and stedfast chief-priest in the things of God, to make propitiation for the sins of the people..." (Hebrews 2:17). Being God and man, Christ was the only one with the ability to perform both tasks. He was the sacrifice and the chief priest. The accomplishment that Christ made for all mankind was on a level mightier than any other. Let us be grateful for the victory over death and the ultimate sacrifice of our Lord and Savior, Jesus Christ. God's plan came to fruition (Isaiah 53).

Christ was the first to live after His sacrifice for sin was made. He was the only person with the power to release the grasp of spiritual and physical death. Consequentially, Jesus died physically, but not spiritually. His Spirit was with His Father and He never sinned. Our sin garnered a place for us in Hell. Without Christ's payment for our sins, God would have been bound to exact that payment from us. Thankfully, Jesus went instead. Jesus' soul never died, because He was never spiritually dead. On the cross, His flesh took the punishment for sin physically and died. His soul rose, and then His body. Jesus was given the authority and commanded by His Father to lay down His life and again to take it (John 10:18).

Christ defeated the power of sin for us on the cross and the second death as His soul rose from Hades (Acts 2:31). This gave way for the human spirit to live freely with Christ. Therefore, Jesus' death and resurrection overcame the death of the spirit, the soul, and the body. Although the Spirit of God and Soul of Christ never died, ours might. His suffering freed us all from a life of sin, and His visit to Hades freed the trapped souls. Jesus' liberation enabled souls to escape the penalty of death in Hell. Finally, His bodily resurrection completed His victory over physical death to unite His Spirit, Soul and Body.

Before Jesus lived on earth as a man, as today, the dead were destined for either Heaven or Hell. If God were their Father, then they would have loved Jesus (John 8:42) who freed their souls from Hades. They were divided into two groups: those in the safety of Hades and those in across the abyss. Death and Hades were to be thrown into the pit (Revelation 20:14). So, in Hades those with Abraham were separated from God the Father's presence, but not His love. These captives in Hades were spared from the suffering of God's eternal wrath and found solace in Abraham's bosom.

THE CONSCIENCE OF GOD

According to John 10:30, Jesus and the Father were considered one. So, knowingly or unknowingly the relationship the departed had with the Father included Jesus. In the wilderness, to Moses, all were baptized in the cloud and in the sea (I Corinthians 10:1-3). Christ was following the Hebrews in the wilderness, and they drank from Him as their spiritual rock (I Corinthians 10:4). Also, see: Exodus 13:21-22.

Due to the fact that false gods were worshipped, God made a provision to overlook the sin of idolatry until Christ came (Acts 17:30). Idolatry was pervasive in the ancient world and today. In Judges 17, Micah observed Jewish customs and possessed idols. God, in His infinite wisdom, sent a Levite to live with Micah and blessed his home. Respectively, Athens was inundated with idolatry, and God sent Paul to minister to the Athenians. Apostle Paul identified the unknown God worshipped by the Athenians as the God who made the world and all things. He indicated that the people were not far from God as His offspring and warned them not to think of God as gold, silver, stone or any artwork of man. Paul told them of one who returned from the dead and would judge the world in righteousness (Acts 17:23-31). So, God fostered awareness of Himself revealed by His servants to complete His work. Notice this unknown Athenian God did not have a name and should not be misconstrued as a blanket acceptance of all religions or gods as a path to Jesus and eternal life.

God made provision for the dead and the living to accept Jesus. All the freed souls in Hades had the opportunity to see and to love Jesus. With Christ's atoning death on the cross for all sin, His descent into Hades brought forgiveness to those there, because Jesus was the only door for all human beings to be saved (John 10:7-9). After this time, the decision to believe and to receive Christ's free gift of salvation and payment for sin had to be made while living.

Many historical figures from the Bible have been heralded for their faith. Abraham and Sarah, in particular, have been praised from the Old Testament to the New. In Hebrews, Sarah was hailed for her faith, because she judged God faithful to keep His promise (Hebrews 11:11). What incredible strength and courage Sarai (Sarah) showed to endure the wilderness, to be held in the Pharaoh's house, and to wait many years for the promise of a son. Sarai's faith held fast throughout adversity. Ultimately, God gave Abraham and Sarah the promise of a son and He honored their faith. They both knew God would perform it and this was declared righteousness (Genesis 15:6 and Romans 4:22).

Walking in love, as Christ loves, shows our works to the perfection of our faith. For example, the positions of husbands and wives represent Christ and the Church. Many, incorrectly, use the word of God to subjugate women rather than build up and edify the members. Husbands are the heads of wives. All men are not the heads of all women. Husbands are to lead in the protection and care of their wives and families. Let men who marry take rightful positions as husbands and women as wives. God has us all under His authority and we must be mindful to fear God while serving in either capacity. Christ is our Rock, we depend on Him to be unwavering in His authority. A husband cannot be Christ, but uses Christ as the example for his leadership role in the family treating his wife as himself. The wife reverences her husband, treating him with respect and together they govern their household as God directs. That direction should always come from God.

Circumventing conflicting moral practices, believers must marry fellow believers in Christ. The husband gives himself for his wife to make her spotless and blameless. Thus setting the example for the family to follow by loving and cherishing the position of the wife. Just as believers in Christ are to honor each other, considering the other first (Philippians 2:3-4), as God's wife; protecting rather than dominating. Christ never bullies nor demeans His wife, the Church, rather submitting to the will of the Father and dying for her.

Let us honor and cherish all people, but especially bear the burdens of our fellow sisters and brothers in Christ. If you know anyone who is being abused get involved. Call the authorities and report the abuser, immediately. Waiting for someone else to act is a cowardly response. Hoping for the abusers to move away or for someone to die is irresponsible and unconscionable. Personally, I needed protection for my safety and for my children from my ex-husband. In the past, I also called the police to help a neighbor and nothing was done to the abuser. A few months later, the woman was found dead in a dumpster. I continue my campaign to persuade lawmakers to change local and state laws to help the abused. Finally, I have joined other women to advocate for abused women to let it be known that the laws are too soft on crimes against women and children.

Be one who overcomes fear by bringing attention to abuse and doing something to stop it. Satan would like nothing more than to strip a believer of his/her salvation through fear. If the power and authority of Christ is living and dwelling in you, Act! Remember, "… 'he who is overcoming shall inherit all things, and I will be to him – a God, and he shall be to me – the son, and to fearful, and unsteadfast, and abominable, and murderers, and whoremongers, and sorcerers, and idolaters, and all the liars, their part [is] in the lake that is burning with fire and brimstone, which is a second death' " (Revelation 21:7-8).

As we grow in Christ let us look as God does at the heart and not on the outside as man does with the eyes (I Samuel 16:7). Paul concludes that seeking a crown from God, running the race and mortifying the flesh should be goals in service to the Lord (Colossians 3:3-6). Scripture asks: "and whoever may have the goods of the world, and may view his brother having need, and may shut up his bowels from him -- how doth the love of God remain in him?" (I John 3:17). Also, James 2:16-17 contends: "and any one of you may say to them, 'Depart ye in peace, be warmed, and be filled,' and may not give to them the things needful for the body, what [is] the profit? so also the faith, if it may not have works, is dead by itself."

Satan has succeeded for millennia to minimize women from within and without the body of Christ. The heretical teaching and manufactured reasons for abusing women have persisted long enough. Christ tore down the wall of defeat and oppression to liberate humanity and eliminate cultural barriers. For "there is not here Jew or Greek, there is not here servant nor freeman, there is not here male and female, for all ye are one in Christ Jesus; and if ye are of Christ then of Abraham ye are seed, and according to promise -- heirs" Galatians 3:28-29. Women through the power of God continued to teach, to inspire, to preach, to evangelize, to minister, to witness, to testify, to prophesy, to lead, to proclaim, to help, to profess, to pastor and to do any other righteous work in Jesus' name. Paul said in Philippians 4:3, "and I ask also thee, genuine yoke-fellow, be assisting those women who in the good news did strive along with me, with Clement also, and the others, my fellow-workers, whose names are in the book of life".

Scripture is given for our good: "every Writing is God-breathed, and profitable for teaching, for conviction, for setting aright, for instruction that is in righteousness, that the man of God may be fitted -- for every good work having been completed" II Timothy 3:16-17. Now, we truly can say we are free, men and women, indeed. Christ affords liberty to all (Galatians 5:13). Bondage comes from the Devil. Men and women are called for service to a sovereign God without any independent approval. We know teachers are to be judged more harshly than others (James 3:1) and false prophets to be thrown in the lake of fire. So, it is vital not to rewrite the Word of God, nor hinder His servants, the prophets (Revelation 10:7).

Remember man was made in the likeness of God, a male and a female (Genesis 5:1, 2). We were made for God's purpose. In marriage the matrix, the glue should be God Himself. God established the relationship between wives and husbands to accomplish His righteous goal: " 'Not good for the man to be alone, I do make to him an helper – as his counterpart' " (Genesis 2:18). God essentially gave men and women the same purpose: to glorify Him. To serve through Christ's example, honored God and performed tasks made way for the perfection of our faith.

Deborah, aforementioned, "a woman inspired, wife of Lapidoth…" fulfilled her commission established by God. She prophesied for God and judged the people of Israel. Giving counsel to the King, Deborah instructed Barak the son of Abinoam to go into battle against Sisera, head of the host of Jabin. Before going into battle, Deborah told Barak that God would give Sisera into the hand of a woman. So, not only did Barak know that he was going to defeat his enemy, he was reassured through God's servant, Deborah, that his enemy would be annihilated. Even with all of this information, he refused to go into battle without her (Judges 4:8-9). So, God sent His Word, through a divinely inspired woman, to inform King Barak that his enemy would be killed at the hand of woman. God instrumentally used women to deliver his message and to carryout His work.

John 15:4 tells believers to remain in God, "as the branch is not able to bear fruit of itself…" Know that God is with you as you serve Him by serving others. Seek for God to have a heart after you. Pray for boldness, contentment, zeal, faith, and humility. Like David, say to yourself, "Jehovah is my light and my salvation, Whom do I fear? Jehovah is the strength of my life, Of whom am I afraid?" (Psalm 27:1) Now, more than ever, embracing the teaching of my parents has helped me to cope with the difficulties of life. Growing up, my mother taught us that our bodies were God's temples. My father used to say to my sister and me, "Girls, be anything you want to be." My mother would say, "As long as you've done your best, that's all we ask." What an incredible gift and example for two wonderful people to leave their children. My mother and father had their faults, but they taught us to love ourselves as individuals, to respect authority and to help those in need. My mother taught us to honor God.

My parents were intellectuals of the highest caliber. Their priority was the educational development of their children and they placed value in things of substance. So, we didn't have to go "find ourselves", because our parents taught us how to explore the good things in life, rather than trying to prove our worth. Regardless of the racial conflicts and prejudice we experienced, innately, we had a sense of purpose and motivation to succeed.

As children growing up, we were encouraged, sometimes compelled, to engage in the usual activities: attending church services, visiting the library and going to school. Besides traveling, playing outside and wresting in the den, for fun, we spent our time reading, listening to music, engaging in stimulating conversation, playing musical instruments, sports, and going to social events. Personally, I had an interest in art and my mom purchased art kits for me to explore those creative outlets.

As a parent, I have learned to listen to my children more and care about what they have to say. Resisting the urge to command obedience, I have worked toward dialogue and a calmer demeanor when resolving problems. Modulating habits to be in tune with Christ has given me an opportunity to show my children their importance.

I hope my children pattern Christ and follow His command to love others, as themselves. My prayer is for them to maintain this behavior for a life-long journey, embracing lives for Christ and rejecting all else. By building up my children with words of strength, rather than criticism, I seek to bless them and foster confidence, trust and a commitment to Godly living. Ultimately my goal is to exemplify a righteous life-style to show my children how Christ, our Rock, changes me and offers us all a place to go for guidance in a time of need or celebration.

As we seek to build a solid foundation in Christ, know that evil persists. Unfortunately, opposition to God's love comes in myriad forms and dimensions. Deception and manipulation are antithetical to God's Kingdom and His order. Witchcraft/sorcery and occult practices use hexes, spells, amulets, etc. to evoke fear, to coerce and to curse people. God has no part in such practices. In fact, Jesus commands us to bless and not curse. "Bless those persecuting you; bless, and curse not" (Romans 12:14). Let all evil be anathema. Witchcraft/sorcery, false prophecy, lying, blasphemy (speaking evil of God and using His name as nothing or cursing God), pornography, drug addiction, sex addiction, adultery, fornication, unbiblical sexuality and homosexuality, horoscopes, numerology, tarot cards, fortune telling, ouija boards, levitation, séances, necromancy (communicating with the dead), riotous living (uncontrolled partying), drunkenness, palm reading, gossip, murder (malicious taking of life, taking innocent life and abortion), Masons and Masonic groups (Shriners, who are Masons), Jesters (Masons known to rape and commit other demonic acts), magick (not the harmless magic, but the evil form of magic that uses demonic powers) and all unrighteous practices are abominable (Please see: Deuteronomy 18:9-14, there are many sources in the Bible denouncing sexual impurity, witchcraft and other demonic practices. The Masonic orders, female counterparts and other secret societies pledge oaths that are forsaken by God. These groups are not in any shape or form Christian, no matter how much they read the Bible).

It is never too late to turn away from the above practices and embrace the abundance that God has. With God's help, we are able to begin new campaigns to serve Him. The word of God says, " 'he who is overcoming shall inherit all things, and I will be to him – a God, and he shall be to me – the son, and to the fearful, and unsteadfast, and abominable, and murderers, and whoremongers, and sorcerers, and idolaters, and all the liars, their part [is] in the lake that is burning with fire and brimstone, which is the second death'" (Revelation 21:7-8).

Killing the Goliath in Us

Inspired by Candace Heyward. As a child, my daughter wanted to hear about David's battle with Goliath and killing him (the good part, according to Candace).

Has your Goliath died? Have you disposed of the formidable foe impeding your growth to fulfill God's plan? In our walk as believers we need to ask questions. If I continue to do what God says is wrong, will I have a place in Heaven? Let us allow the Bible to answer these questions. Mentioned earlier, David's involvement with Bathsheba was an abuse of his authority. Upon impregnating her, David ordered her husband, Uriah, to return home from the battlefield. Uriah's refusal to enjoy the comforts of home, while the other men fought, unraveled David's scheme to unite Uriah with his wife, Bathsheba. David attempted and failed to conceal the true identity of the baby's father. In a cold-blooded decision, David sent orders to place Uriah into the heat of battle to be abandoned and overcome by Bene-Ammon.

We know David repented and was forgiven (II Samuel 12:13); however, the damage reverberated beyond his kingdom. The extent of David's sin caused God's enemies to blaspheme God (II Samuel 12:14). Also, the defeat of one of God's mighty warriors emboldened them. They stridently opposed the Israelites. So, Uriah's death also contributed to their disregard for God.

Before David ruled, God saved him from the deadly weapon of King Saul. Now, David had taken the life of an innocent man with the sword. Not only did David kill Uriah, but used the Israelites' consummate enemy to fall on him. These selfish actions of David overshadowed all the blessings he had enjoyed. As a result God sent Nathan, the Prophet, to deliver a message to David concerning his son and that his house would be plagued with violence.

Nathan told David his son with Bathsheba would die. In direct contradiction to God's decision, David fasted and prayed for the boy to live. David's petition was refused. Did that mean that the death of his child was a punishment from God? God made a statement to both the Israelites and the Bene-Ammon that He was not in favor of David's actions. However, God lovingly received that child into His arms, as He did and still does for all innocent life lost. As required by the commandments of the Old Testament, a life was taken for a life. God maintained the Law, but He also showed His resolve against unrighteousness.

Remember, God could not contradict His Word and ignore the violation. Taking human life was satisfied with the death of another one. The laws of the Old Testament were in operation, then and now in Christ. The major difference is that Christ's love culminated the satisfaction for all required sacrifices for sin. His death abolished the need for further sacrifices for sin, and thus fulfilled the Law. The uniqueness of Christ's sacrifice brought life to a world of destruction. With the death of Christ, sin was forgiven once forever. The death of Christ was the only substitute for sin to satisfy God's punishment for sin. Jesus ended this practice by being the first, last and only death able to remove sin.

Unfortunately, Goliath mocked God's power and attacked His children. Defeated enemies like Goliath and the youth who threatened Elisha experienced the justice of God. With God's help, David conquered Goliath on the battlefield, and God protected Elisha in the way. As found in II Kings 2:23 boys gathered in a mob behind Elisha. They taunted him to go up and ascend. As we know, earlier, Elijah had been taken to Heaven, and now the boys terrorized Elisha to go up, also. This large crowd of youth, which amassed from a nearby city, posed a significant threat to Elisha. He cursed them in the name of God and two she bears came out of the woods killing 42 of them.

I would never advocate killing children. Apparently, the level of violence perpetuated by the youth caused a severe response from God to mitigate the situation and to protect Elisha. I trust God's righteous decision to determine the weight of their punishment. Throughout the Bible, God's judgments cause the death of many, including children (Numbers 16). This may be easier to understand if factoring in an important variable. Jesus welcomes the innocent and the unborn, because they have not done any good or evil (Romans 9:11). He said that the kingdom of God belongs to such as little children (Matthew 19:14; Luke 18:16; Mark 10:14).

Even though Jesus became sin for all, the wicked have no fear of God (2 Peter 2; Romans 3:22; 2 Corinthians 5:21; Philippians 3:9). So, "Be not led astray; God is not mocked; for what a man may sow – that also he shall reap" (Galatians 6:7). When one thinks he or she is mocking or deriding God, the ill intentions return to the offender. Meaning, the offense to God reflects the lack of respect for God and coincides with the absence of God's blessing, thus a self imposed curse or curses.

Consequently, those practicing sorcery (sorcerers, shamans, psychics, mediums, conjurers, enchanters, witches/warlocks, palm readers, magicians using demonic magic, magick and the like) operate in the supernatural and wickedly imitate the role of God by communicating with the dead, blessing, cursing, predicting the future and other spiritual tasks reserved for His dominion. Since only God truly has the power to righteously rule these operations, those practicing sorcery are deceiving others and falling victim to their own deception.

Even though this power is real and comes from Satan, God gives us choices honoring our individuality. Without the ability to choose good and evil, we could not say God is Love. God represents the epitome of Love by allowing us the option to use our authority. By choosing, we know that we are made in God's image. Gratefully, our spirit is our failsafe. Having the solution in Christ, God has a provision to wipe away the mistakes or sin. Not only does God graciously give us authority over ourselves, we have the life of His only Son. He just asks us to protect our souls by receiving His offer of a free gift of salvation. As our Salvation, Jesus waits for us with His arms wide open.

Further, no one can diminish the character of God, or intimidate Him. In actuality, any attempt to do so opens a spiritual door removing God's protection and brings potentially unbridled harm to the offender(s) as seen in Numbers chapter 16. As believers, we must remind others of the results of deception and attempts to cheat God's people. Attempting to fool the children of God proves futile. Ananias and Sapphira are an example of this. Acts 5:1 records the deception of the husband and wife who both subsequently die for lying about withholding a portion of their gift to the Church.

Aaron's sons brought a strange fire sacrifice to God. By disobeying God, they were in His presence without a covering of protection and died (Leviticus 10:1-2). Another priest, Eli, had sons who were committing abominations at the entrance to the temple. God destroyed them, as well (I Samuel 2:22-34).

Along with the Old Testament covenant punishments, wars between Israel and the inhabitants of the land, given to the Hebrews by God, God Himself carried out death sentences. One could assert that God commanded the Hebrews to kill the inhabitants of the land, but that would be an over simplification. God gave the Israelites the land He promised them. Why did God choose the Hebrews? Obviously, God planned to bring His Son into the world for all of us, through the Jews. God's peremptory judgment established a place for His kingdom on earth, at His return. Any one standing in the way of God's will, including Israelites, were or will be destroyed (Numbers 16; Acts 12:23; Revelation 20:10, 14-15).

The Bible makes it very clear that there are those who erroneously think killing is for the service of God (John 16:2). We know that murderers do not inherit the Kingdom of God. Revelation 21:7-8 tells us "...to fearful, and unstedfast, and abominable, and murderers, and whoremongers, and sorcerers, and idolaters, and all the liars, their part is in the lake that is burning with fire and brimstone, which is a second death.' " Also, a passage from Galatians reveals, "and those who are Christ's, the flesh did crucify with the affections, and the desires" (Galatians 5:24). What are those affections and desires that Christ's brethren crucify? The scriptures list them: "adultery, whoredom, uncleanness, lasciviousness, idolatry, witchcraft, hatred, strifes, emulations, wraths, rivalries, dissensions, sects, envyings, drunkennesses, revellings, and such like, of which I tell you before, as I also said before, that those doing such things the reign of God shall not inherit" (Galatians 5:20-21).

Christ outlined what to hate and what to love. He taught believers to display mercy and gentleness. In fact, Jesus, as God in the flesh, gave His examples to follow. Believers were instructed not to give place to the Devil (Ephesians 4:27). Those who dishonored the Father angered Christ. Examples included: the practices of the moneychangers (Matthew 21:12); the Pharisees' deception of others (Matthew 23:27), and attempts to be a stumbling block to God (Matthew 16:21-23).

THE CONSCIENCE OF GOD

The God of all creation revealed His conscience. God had been making preparations for the coming of His Son, Jesus Christ, Yeshua our Messiah in the flesh. He gave all people a way to recognize right from wrong individually, and set the foundation for the reception of His Son into the heart and mind. Prior to the end of the Old Testament, God gave the Jews a new covenant. God Himself promised to write His statutes and commandments on their hearts and minds. When Jesus refused to let Satan rage unabated, His actions were no surprise. God's scribes, prophets, disciples and apostles recorded His standard in the Bible for living. Jesus expelled demons and cast them into pigs that went over a cliff into the water below (Matthew 8:32; Mark 5:13; Luke 8:33). God was responsible for the death of people, as well. So, how did a loving God kill? This has been established as God keeping His Law. He did not overlook sin (Jeremiah 5:9).

God told Moses, " 'I AM THAT WHICH I AM' "(Exodus 3:14). God was and is sovereign and eternal. In like fashion, Jesus answered the High Priest. "Again the chief priest was questioning him, and saith to him, 'Art thou the Christ – the Son of the Blessed?' and Jesus said, 'I am; and ye shall see the Son of Man sitting on the right hand of the power, and coming with the clouds, of heaven' " (Mark 14:61-62). Jesus said, " 'Verily, verily, I say to you, Before Abraham's coming – I am" (John 8:58). Why, because Jesus saw Abraham in the future. Our eternal God has been, is and will be. "Jesus Christ yesterday and to-day the same, and to the ages" (Hebrews 13:8).

Baptism by Fire

Before moving forward, I must address baptism. Baptism is both physical and spiritual. Water baptism is an outward expression acknowledging that Christ washes away sin. In the Gospels, John the Baptist baptizes with water. It has no bearing on the salvation of the individual. However, the believer may want to be baptized as a result of their conversion and remember the event to foster personal growth in Christ. In turn, God may use this time to encourage others to repent from sin. As believers, water baptism publicly expresses new life in Christ. Let us remember, on the cross, Jesus tells the thief he will join Him in Paradise and allows the thief into Heaven without water baptism. Moreover, Christ tells the repentant thief, " 'Verily I say to thee, To-day with me thou shalt be in the paradise' " (Luke 23:43). The Holy Spirit baptizes with fire (Mark 1:8; Acts 2; Acts 11:15-16). Also, Mark 1:4 expresses the need for baptism of repentance for the forgiveness of sin.

Not focusing on the outer appearance of a person and the eyes, God directs His attention to matters of the heart (I Samuel 16:7). Let us remember Jesus' death is for us, a corrupt and unscrupulous lot, remember only God is good (Mark 10:18). On the cross, the thief humbly petitions Jesus and receives his forgiveness. So, while we all sin (Romans 3:23) requiring salvation, there is hope for us "that if thou mayest confess with thy mouth the Lord Jesus, and mayest believe in thy heart that God did raise him out of the dead, thou shalt be saved" (Romans 10:9).

Although water baptism is a public declaration of ones faith to follow Christ, admission to Heaven is only through forgiveness of sin and professing Jesus as the Savior alive from the dead. The practical application of water baptism gives believers an opportunity to declare their faith, make a symbolic break from sin to feel clean inside and to profess Jesus without any shame of the Gospel. Water baptism represents the cleansing power of God, Christ's resurrection from the dead and illustrates the victory of Christ over the death of sin, the bonds of Hell and the hold of the grave. Consequently, those who have or will undergo the practice of water baptism are still required to have a change of heart and obtain salvation through Jesus Christ.

In Matthew 3:11, John has described water baptism as a starting point for change to reformation and the baptism Jesus will bring to believers. " 'I indeed do baptize you with water to reformation, but he who after me is coming is mightier than I, of whom I am not worthy to bear the sandals, he shall baptize you with the Holy Spirit and with fire, whose fan [is] in his hand, and he will thoroughly cleanse his floor, and will gather his wheat to the storehouse, but the chaff he will burn with fire unquenchable.' "

Jesus told the disciples that they would drink of the same cup and experience his baptism (Matthew 20:23; Mark 10:38). It was not until Jesus' death and ascension that the Holy Spirit baptized with fire. The Book of Acts vividly depicted baptism by fire. The believers in Christ were fluently speaking languages other than those native to them. God signified this as the baptism by fire with flames appearing above their heads. Speaking in tongues of men and angels represented the presence of the Holy Spirit.

The manifestation of the Holy Spirit came in the form of proclamation and prophecy, as well. For example, when Mary visited Elizabeth, the babe (John the Baptist) leapt in Elizabeth with joy. Full of the Spirit, Elizabeth knew that Mary was carrying the Lord. She blessed the baby and blessed Mary for believing and for being the mother of the Messiah. Also, Elizabeth prophesied that all the Lord's Words to Mary would be complete (Luke 1:41-45).

Elizabeth's husband, Zacharias was full of the Holy Spirit, also. On the eighth day and circumcision of John the Baptist, Zacharias began to prophesy of God's blessing concerning the redemption of His people, the salvation in the house of David, His servant, and relief from their enemies (Luke 1:68-74). Also, Zacharias said his son was to be called God's Prophet of the Most High, who was to go before the face of the Lord and prepare His ways (Luke 1: 76).

When God anointed Saul, the Holy Spirit was in operation, also. In I Samuel 10:10, the presence of the Holy Spirit moved Saul to prophesy with a group of prophets. These references showed the work of the

Holy Spirit, but not the baptism by fire. This action took place after Jesus' departure, and the expression of the Holy Spirit or the Comforter came (John 16:7).

Tithing and Offering

Now, addressing the idea of first fruits and giving the first of everything to God. Many believers debate over tithes and offering. Matthew 6:33 states, " Seek ye first the kingdom of God and His righteousness and all these things shall be added unto you". The first step is to seek the kingdom of God, God's righteousness. God's Kingdom is similar to the miniscule mustard seed that grows into a large tree and provides shelter, or leaven that completely transforms dough (Luke 13:19, 21). Be like God and live a life that exemplifies and glorifies Him. "His kingdom is at hand" (Mark 1:15). You have access to Heaven on earth (Matthew 3:2). The angels, Jesus, the Father and the Holy Spirit advocate a single purpose: God's will. Righteousness reveals the believers' integrity to do the will of God. We should take care of the orphans and the widows in their affliction, while keeping ourselves free from the stains of the world. James calls this pure religion (James 1:27). As believers we should visit the sick and imprisoned. Also, we should not blame others for their situation, but help them and give them all that they require until they no longer have a need (Deuteronomy 15:7-8). These are the sacrifices that God expects from believers and this is where our tithes and offering should go directly and indirectly.

The Conscience

Every person has a conscience and is accountable to God. Believers recognize the need for God who in turn places His laws inside their hearts and minds (Hebrews 10:16 and Jeremiah 31:31). Conversely believers align with God's laws and nonbelievers to their own devices. So, the state of the conscience dictates the choices someone makes. For our purposes, using the ability and desire to do what one deems right and wrong constitutes having a conscience. A corrupt conscience becomes unable to discern such. When one continues to sin, the end result is death. Justifying and perpetuating misdeeds corrupts the conscience. For God, this is impossible. This is why seeking God and His righteousness results in eternal life. The conscience of God reveals the character of God. He guides all to judge with righteous judgment (John 7:24).

When we make choices to please the flesh, we sin. Sowing to the flesh reaps corruption (Galatians 6:7-8). These are not desires to satisfy innocuous personal taste or preference, but ones that are clearly in opposition to God's Word. We sin when we disobey God and turn God's truth into a lie. The scripture, Romans 1:25, shows us the end results of twisting God's truth. Here persons become idolaters, by changing God's incorruptible glory into the corruptible images of man, birds, beasts walking on all four feet and reptiles (Romans 1:23).

First, counterfeiting God's truth results in vile affections: women change their natural use, which is against nature, and men lust after one another. Consequently, the soul is unable to abide in Christ's ways. This is not worth giving up eternal life with Christ in Heaven. Press into Christ, fall at Christ's feet and cry out to Him for help, because His salvation is the only free gift that will last forever.

Our witness is a standard by which nonbelievers measure Christ. So, we must curse the evil and embrace the good exercising our authority to bind on earth and have it bound in Heaven. This way we are powerful to fulfill our commitment to Christ by walking as brethren in faith. As others, learn to sing a song of joy and give God praise to find the worth in suffering with Him. Enduring the struggle for Christ is a testament to the resilience of God in us. As ironic as it may seem, one's suffering may be the very thing that causes the offender to see a need for change. Of course, it feels good to respond in kind and get a vengeful lick in, but Jesus tells us to turn the other cheek.

Second, fear is the other weapon Satan uses against believers. My best offense and defense is the truth. You may not have time to do more than pray quickly and respond, but respond in love. By walking in the Spirit we produce the fruit of the Spirit: love, joy, peace, kindness, meekness, long suffering, goodness, temperance, faith. Silently praying to God and watching Him diffuse a situation is mind-blowing. As mentioned earlier, calling on the angels to fight for you is another way to move Satan out of the way. Staying steadfast in your resolve unmoved by fear is to be more than a conqueror. Victorious in Christ, as the temple of God, we are His treasure. As God treats us with dignity and respect, we must value ourselves. Often, I minister to people as God instructs, and then walk away. God speaks to me in many ways: directly, through other believers, situations, His creation and His written word. As believers, our words hold tremendous weight and our witness is most important.

In order to look more closely at the conscience, let us discuss faith and salvation. The letter to the Hebrews highlights the works of Abraham, Rahab, Sarah, and others, but those works do not give salvation. Their deeds reflect the acceptance of God. Salvation is an extension of God's grace through His work. We know faith without works is dead (James 2:17, 20 and 26), and Jesus offers to bless us through His acts of love.

To obtain Salvation, our acceptance of God's love through the sacrifice of Jesus Christ on the cross has to be recognized in our hearts. Consequently, the fruit declared by John revealed the necessary actions of true believers. Shown in our appreciation for God and acknowledgment of His love, believers serve God by serving others and doing the work of God to build the temple (James 1:22; II Kings 22:5).

So, is it possible for believers to sin? David's life shows that this is the case. Falling prey to sin, David being a man after God's heart overcomes many evil situations. Then, you may ask, "What's the point?" What's the point in believing in God and trying to be holy, if you're just going to fail?" The difference is between sin and iniquity. Although, we have a sin nature to transgress against God's will, we do not have to sin continually and habitually. Continuing to repeat sin is falling into iniquity. This pattern of behavior must be avoided to prevent a hardening of the heart and a searing of the conscience. As believers, we have that conscience in us from God. We now, through Christ, have access to salvation in the secret of the new man (read Ephesians 2:15). This is the place God inhabits.

With God as our hope, and help, to avoid falling, we need to possess: humility, faith, boldness, contentment and zeal. Having humility to reach out to Him, believers must be steadfast while making Godly choices (2 Peter 1:10). "God who is quickening the dead, and is calling the things that be not as being" (Romans 4:17), equips believers to be wise and to think according to the measure of faith God gives (Romans 12:3).

When we possess boldness, as David, we are able to face and kill Goliaths. Let us have contentment, like Paul, to abound and to be abased for the Lord. May my mother's zeal for God burn in me to love God with a jealous passion and to serve Him with all of my heart.

The scripture shows us that those living in the flesh are unable to please God (Romans 8:8). Years ago God told me, "If you continue on the path that you are on, you will not return". I was in iniquity and needed to change my behavior or relinquish my salvation. Paul spoke very directly to his brethren, fellow believers, about their destructive behavior. In Galatians chapter 5, we see that the brethren were attacking each other and would all have been destroyed. They were forfeiting their inheritance in the Kingdom of God by committing works of the flesh. "And manifest also are the works of the flesh, which are: Adultery, whoredom, uncleanness, lasciviousness, idolatry, witchcraft, hatred, strifes, emulations, wraths, rivalries, dissensions, sects, envyings, murders, drunkennesses, revellings, and such like, of which I tell you before, as I also said before, that those doing such things the reign of God shall not inherit" (Galatians 5:19-21). Also see: Deuteronomy 18; Romans 1:29; I Corinthians 6:9-10; Revelation 22:15.

Reading further in Galatians chapter 5, one sees the need to walk in the Spirit and not in the flesh. Also, the saving grace of God is a gift. By receiving that gift, one also receives salvation. We may reject that gift and find ourselves without an inheritance. This is why I am choosing to write this book. As I am free, I want others to live without deception. We belong to God. So, why then do some turn away from Christ? The answer lies in conversion. Jesus asserts this need to Peter. A change of heart allows one to turn away permanently from the propensity to sin, to be selfless, abandoning worthless desires. It is then, that God is able to seal us forever. Giving oneself totally to God for His benefit brings about this permanent conversion. This is overcoming.

In Luke 22:31-32, Peter was eventually converted. Previously, Peter knew Jesus was the Christ our Messiah, but had not given himself wholly to Christ, even though the Holy Spirit revealed the true identity of Jesus to him. Jesus told Peter that the Holy Spirit had revealed that truth to him, but Peter still allowed Satan to use him. For this reason Jesus told Peter if he did not let Him wash his feet that he would have nothing to do with Him. Just like Peter and all believers, total control had to be given to God.

That conversion must be completely finished in the life of the believer. Jesus finished His work on the cross (John 19:30), and completed His task to die for our sin. He then rose from the dead. That signified to the believer to be holy, and separate from the world, to be a true believer who walks in the Spirit to inherit the kingdom of God (Romans 12:2).

Through the willingness of a believer, God brings about change in a person's life. Uniquely Christian, this is the only religion that worships a living God who offers forgiveness for sin without demanding payment from the worshipper. Christ paid the price for sin on the cross. The problem occurs when sin is continual and becomes iniquity. This has the potential to permanently sever the covenant between God and the believer. Iniquity causes the soul to become callous and unaffected by the need of the human spirit to unite with God. Falling prey to ungodly doctrine, eventually the soul no longer recognizes him/herself. Good works and self-sacrifice fall short only to become empty and meaningless attempts at happiness. So, as James 1:22-24 instructs, "… become ye doers of the word, and not hearers only deceiving yourselves, because, if any one is a hearer of the word and not a doer, this one hath been like to a man viewing his natural face in a mirror, for he did view himself, and hath gone away, and immediately he did forget of what kind he was...."

Ending the search for happiness rests in being a doer of the Word and not a hearer only. Following James' teaching, we have the opportunity to experience liberty, true freedom by endeavoring to serve God, "and he who did look into the perfect law -- that of liberty, and did continue there, this one -- not a forgetful hearer becoming, but a doer of work -- this one shall be happy in his doing" (James 2:25).

The blood of Jesus cleanses away sin permanently. Human beings lack the essential components to manufacture an awareness of sin. Looking to God for direction, the shed blood of Jesus Christ, the only worthy sacrifice, may save us from Hell. Yes, God always has His arms stretched toward us, but we may reject that gift of His love by choosing our way and not His. Matthew 7:14 reminds us "how strait [is] the gate, and compressed the way that is leading to the life, and few are those finding it!" That is why all religions do not lead to God and entrance into Heaven. Forgiveness is the essential component to eternity in Heaven. The acceptance of fault, as a result of a humble spirit, leads to true repentance. Acknowledging that one needs to be redeemed or purchased back to God and out of the self-serving desires brings about the necessary change. One must come to Christ as a little child (Matthew 18:3). Like children, being inquisitive and willing to learn, allows one to experience the hope of salvation. A confidence to be blessed by God comes from believing in the power of God and residing in His Son Jesus and risen Savior.

Making mistakes is human; receiving the Messiah takes divine courage. Believers in Christ have the humility to admit their transgressions. Also, this unique Christian attribute of forgiveness entitles ALL unrestricted access to the inheritance of the kingdom of God and Heaven. The kingdom of God is near (Matthew 3:2; Matthew 4:7). Jesus Christ opens the door as the Way for us to stand without condemnation before the Father, forgiven of sin.

How important is it for all to understand the freedom of the spirit and the soul. The spirit converses with God apart from the soul. Our spirits give us a means with which to directly communicate with God. Our souls represent the unique personalities we have from God. Given that we each have a spirit and a soul, we have a future eternal life or death. With our souls we think (question, reason, surmise, etc.). Admittance to either Heaven or Hell is in our hands (see Matthew 25). After we die we will be aware. Without Christ, the soul will comprehend that he/she is in Hell without any way of escape. The person knows that the spirit and the body are without the comfort of peace God offers. At death the liberty to choose one's destiny ends. How terrible it is to think about the spirit and the soul being in perpetual confinement, unable to be free from the torment of Hell. Communication with God is to become only vile cursing with the smell of stench and unfathomable pain forever.

This is why it is vitally important to seek God, now. Studying the Word reveals key tools for spiritual growth. Be diligent to ask questions and to gain knowledge, to have a better understanding of God and to know the Word of God. Just as Psalm 128 teaches us the wife is like a vine producing fruit when her husband fears the Lord. Meaning the husband who is obedient to God has a wife who has the opportunity to grow and blossom as God's daughter. An obedient husband supplies the home with stability and gives a wife the necessary energy to bear fruit as the vine. He also has sons [children] who are as olive plants around his table. That is the image of Christ, Jesus our husband and friend to the Church.

Seeking to gratify a need through excessive behavior, as a way to satisfy unfulfilled desires will not last, but leave an even bigger hole. How does a person overcome these unrelenting desires to sin? Here's a little secret God shared with me. Come to an end of yourself. Have such a hatred for the way you behave that you must change. Make the desire to change greater than the one to sin. Be bold to tell yourself the truth. Say, "You just don't want to change. You enjoy being the way you are". Then, turn to God; admit that you are the cause of your failure and pain. Get alone with God and put your face on the floor. Before the Lord lie prostrate, refuse to move until you are changed, and let God take it from there. When you are in Christ, you will have the well of living water springing up from you that satisfies thirst forever (John 4:14).

Well, to elaborate on the secret, we need to be at the end of our wants, before we can do the will of God. That is dying to the flesh. Put whatever you are struggling with before God and ask Him to solve the problem. The scripture, Philippians 4:6, says not to be anxious, but instead be in prayer, thankful, and tell God what you want. With humility and contentment make the petition. God will help you.

It's akin to being without care or not being anxious (Philippians 4:6). Just like Jesus sleeping in the boat during the storm. Throwing caution to the wind? No. Consider following David's example. Even though Saul is mercilessly pursuing David in an effort to kill him, David continues to elude Saul. In pursuit, Saul stops to relieve himself in a cave. What Saul doesn't know is that David is hiding in the same cave. Going undetected, David is able to cut Saul's clothes (I Samuel 24). Once again, God puts Saul in David's hand by placing Saul and his men in a deep sleep. This allows David to take Saul's spear and cruse of water (I Samuel 26:12). God gives David boldness to face danger and faith to know God's protection is unwavering. By serving God and refusing to harm Saul, God's anointed (I Samuel 26:11), David adorns himself in zeal for God. Even when Saul is on the verge of catching David, he has contentment to accept God's will. After David escapes he appeals to Saul with humility to cease his violent pursuit. Also, David reminds Saul that God judges between them and rescues him from Saul's hand (I Samuel 24).

Often, God provided for David. Although David made mistakes, he repented and got back on track. Even while fleeing for his life from Saul, he remained faithful to God. Twice David had motive and opportunity to kill Saul. Fearing God, David refused to harm Saul, because God had anointed him (I Samuel 24:6; I Samuel 26:9, 11, 12). David even fed his men bread intended for the priests. Giving the priests' bread to the soldiers was forbidden (I Samuel 21). They were hungry and the priest allowed the men to have the bread, if they kept themselves from women. David was very cleaver. He told Ahimelech as he was taking the bread that the men would have kept themselves from women. So, from David's departure with bread to the men, he knew that there was too little time for them to be with women. This allowed David to say that the men would have been without women and holy to receive the priests' bread (I Samuel 21).

I truly believe that that illuminated why David was a man after God's heart. David was flawed, as everyone else, but he completed every task

God gave him. David constantly gave thanks and praise, blessing God. When he was in trouble he conferred with God. He refused to forfeit his inheritance. He knew he was a lowly sinner who feared God. So much so, when God commanded His prophet Nathan to go and have a talk with David, he was able, through creative means, to correct David, the king. David had taken away Uriah's precious wife, Bathsheba (II Samuel 12:1-12), but was angered when told of a man's only choice sheep taken by a wealthy man. As David soon learned, Nathan was referring to him and said, "You are that man" (II Samuel 12:7).

The conscience of God weighs right and wrong. The decision to take a life, preserve or renew it is perfect in God. Being in the image of God, each human possesses a spirit. It is this spirit that New Age thought often misconstrues as a collective conscience or being a part of God. Like God: Father, Son, Holy Spirit, we have three parts: a soul, body and spirit (I Thessalonians 5:23). The spirit allows us to communicate directly with God, independent of our soul. Note, our soul communicates with God, as well. When one part of the person is communicating with God or simultaneously with the other parts, they bear witness along with the feelings of the body.

When a person's behavior resembles that of uninhibited animals, his or her conscience is corrupt. An example of this is found in Numbers 25:8. The Bible depicts God's reaction and anger toward His chosen people, the Israelites, who are committing idolatry, fornication and eating sacrifices to other gods. Also, when Phinehas kills the Israelite and the Midianite woman, his actions stay the plague of fornication (Numbers 25:8). Today, most would consider this type of law enforcement barbaric. Later, we see Jesus bringing a different approach to deal with fornication, but the ultimate consequence for continuing in sin, then and now, is still death. Though disease may cause the initial physical death, ultimately the death of the spirit and soul in Hell is the result of sin.

Like the rich man, habitual refusal to help someone in need, caused a hardening of the heart (Luke 16:19-31). Pharaoh's heart hardened over time as he defied God (Exodus 7:14; 8:32). This occurred even though God showed the Egyptians His power (Exodus 14:18). The disregard for the work of the Spirit of God, not only led to the hardness of the heart, but consequently the corruption of the conscience.

The story of the Good Samaritan gives a perfect example of following the Spirit of God (Luke 10:30-37). Through deliberate actions, we dictate the path of our souls. As human beings with souls, spirits and bodies, we have the inevitable future of life after death. Some, like Elijah, have the experience of translation (leaving their bodies without a physical death).

By making lifestyle choices that please God, our efforts mandate a healthy spiritual relationship with God and others. So, it is the soul that governs the eternal resting place and chooses whether or not to serve God (Joshua 24:15). Since God has no desire for any one to die in Hell (Ezekiel 33:11; II Peter 3:8-10), He enables the soul to choose life and provides our spirits with a direct link to Him.

In preparation for God's Spirit to dwell in us, we are made as three in one. The outer court, for all things to enter; the inner court, with restricted access; and the holy of holies, reserved for the High Priest, Jesus. Each part has a separate function just like God the Father, God the Spirit and God the Son. Being the first born and first fruits the beginning of a sacrifice from the dead (Colossians 1:18; I Corinthians 15:20; see: http://biblehub.com/lexicon/1_corinthians/15-20.htm), Jesus is the only sacrifice to die sin and live again.

Prior to His death, Jesus promises to rebuild the temple in three days. Referring to His body, Jesus shows His intentions to place His Spirit in the flesh of all who would believe, as well. This is how God prepares each person to receive His spirit. The body represents the outer court, the soul or inner court and the spirit or holy of holies. As a person receives Jesus Christ as Savior for forgiveness of sin, the Spirit of God comes inside to dwell or abide in her or him (I Corinthians 3:16).

Consequently, now the soul has to go through a conversion. Many believers often have a difficult time changing. This process requires God's assistance, Godly oversight, fellowship, personal Bible devotions and prayer. Reflecting the love God has for us exhibits the growth of our maturity in Christ for others to pattern. Apostle Paul mentions this struggle and tells the reader to seek a mind like God's by putting away childish things. As mature believers we must no longer want milk, but solid food (I Corinthians 3:2). Being satisfied knowing that Jesus died for our sins is not enough to grow as a Christian. We must act upon the desires that God places in our hearts. Having zeal to promote God's Word encourages us to have love for one another. As we walk with humility in gentleness, let us exhibit the boldness of Christ to speak the truth.

The reverberating effects of breaking God's covenant were recorded in Jeremiah 22, and Deuteronomy 31:26-29, when Moses warned the Israelites. Jeremiah 22:2-6 indicated that ignoring the plight of the needy and forsaking the Lord's covenant slated Judah for destruction. Through Jeremiah, God warned Judah's kings to exercise judgment, to live righteously, to deliver the oppressed, to refrain from shedding innocent blood; neither to oppress nor to wrong the sojourner, orphan and widow (Jeremiah 22:1-5). Despite God's instructions, the kings honored their own wishes and fell at the hands of their enemies. Jerusalem was in ruins, because the inhabitants bowed to other gods and served them (v. 9). God resigned Shallum, son of King Josiah, to die in a foreign land (vv. 11,12). Jehoiakim built his house by unrighteous means. After his neighbor performed a service, he withheld his wages (v. 13). Also, he committed acts of oppression and violence, shed innocent blood and focused on dishonest gain (v. 17). He was to have the undignified burial of an ass (v. 19). Coniah (Jehoiachin), son of Jehoiakim, whom God regarded as a seal on His right hand (v. 24), received what he feared. He and his mother were to find destruction by the hands of their enemies, the Chaldeans and King Nebuchadrezzar of Babylon. Longing to return home they were to die in a foreign land (v. 27). God relegated Coniah and his offspring to live in a foreign land (v.28). Also, God said to write him childless, a man who was not to prosper in his days and none of his offspring were to proper, to sit on the throne of David and to rule again in Judah (v. 30).

Contradicting and pushing God away risks breaking any covenant we have with Him. Thwarting His will by embracing our own sets us up for a dissatisfied life of emptiness we are unable to fill. What seems right to man the end is death (Proverbs 14:12; 16:25). Since we know our actions reflect the fertility of the heart, the same concerns sin. When we conceive sin in our hearts and minds we die spiritually. To break free from this perpetual sinful state of being, all believers must go through a process of turning or conversion.

When Peter converted, he sought God's will and His righteousness.

THE CONSCIENCE

Jesus said, " ...' Simon, Simon, lo, the Adversary did ask you for himself to sift as the wheat, and I besought for thee, that thy faith may not fail; and thou, when thou didst turn, strengthen thy brethren' " (Luke 22:31-32). Jesus prayed for Peter, and He desired for us to serve each other. Being tempted was not a sin. When a person acted on the desire in thought or in deed that was what killed the soul and spirit. This propensity to sin had to be overcome only through Christ. He will send ministering angels. Just ask.

Desiring to see the body of Christ free from erring, due to false teaching, and living righteously before God, I implore every believer to examine her or his state. If you are living with a girlfriend or a boyfriend, using drugs or disobeying God in any way, it's time to turn and be converted. God will make a provision for your righteous decision to repent. My mother told me when you start having sex it's hard to stop. Pray for God to take away whatever has a hold on you. Take the time to lie on your face before God, seek deliverance and refuse to get up until God releases you. When you reach the end of yourself, petition God to give you a new start.

When David petitioned God to save his ailing son, he had lain before God for days. This prayer was in direct contradiction to God's decision (II Samuel 12:14). God told David, through the prophet, that his son was going to die. Remember God asked Abram to sacrifice Isaac, and he did obey. Thankfully, God spared Isaac. Also, Abram, now Abraham (Genesis 18:16-33), asked God for the righteous would he spare Sodom? God did not, but only allowed Lot, who was righteous (II Peter 2:7), to leave with his family beforehand. Concerning the death of David and Bathsheba's son, regardless of David's righteousness, God preserved His will. This mandated God's decision to allow the sickness to claim the life of the child. Regrettably, David's sin resulted in a terrible outcome.

Job expressed the things of God as too wonderful to understand (Job 42:3). That sentiment through suffering afforded Job an opportunity to see the curious nature of God. Perhaps if David's ailing son had lived he would have become king, instead of Solomon. This may have prevented the building of the temple or fulfilling God's plan for the Messiah. At all cost, Jesus had to die for the sins of the world. Nothing was to impede the will of God and only God knew the consequences for allowing the child to live. At the time it was difficult to see, but they were in God's will and Christ's grace was to come (Ephesians 2:7-8).

Conversely, why did God extend Hezekiah's life after sending word by the prophet that it was time for him to die? The reason lay in the righteousness of Hezekiah. He cried out to God and relied on his clean record in exchange for his life. God accepted the plea and granted Hezekiah's petition. Relative to David, he gave the enemies an opportunity to blaspheme or spurn God. His actions were forgiven, but the death of his son was inevitable. Was God harsh to bless one while refusing another? No, He sovereignty took control. His actions coincided with His Word. Focused on changing our actions rather than God's, we have been reassured that God decision was just.

If God sacrifices His own, to eliminate sin, nothing may spare us from His wrath. God's will is final. To think that we have the last say in a matter with God, by being stubborn and defiant, deteriorates our relationship with Him. My former pastor is in retirement, but here is a passage from his previous sermon: " We desire what we want; God has what we need. God wants to give us more than we want, but we give it up for something less." Pastor Josh Lively, March 14, 2010. Pastor Josh is speaking of the Reubenites and the Gadites who give up their inheritance of the Promised Land, refusing to settle across the Jordan River, but instead choose to stay on the Eastern side of the river.

The Scriptures tell us that power and strength come from God. "He is giving power to the weary, And to those not strong, He increaseth might" (Isaiah 40:29). As believers who have access to the same strength in Christ, we must encourage and strengthen each other. Having fellowship with other believers, our conversation and behavior should reflect a standard pleasing to God. As believers inheriting the reign of God, we produce the fruit of the Spirit: "Love, joy, peace, longsuffering, kindness, goodness, faith, meekness, temperance…" (Galatians 5:22 and 23). (Please study prautes. This is the Greek word for meekness.)

Speaking of strength, the husband is commanded by God to cleave, hang-on, to his wife (Genesis 2:24). As the husband is instructed by God to cling to the wife, his prayers are hindered when he offends her (I Peter 3:7). As the body houses the soul of a believer, with God's help, the husband and wife become one flesh (Matthew 10:8) and must work in tandem to maintain the soul of the marriage. Even when there is nothing apparent to give, the wife, as a result of having an obedient husband, stocks the storehouse with provision for the family. This is the fruit of Psalm 128.

Both have essential roles in God's service to secure the marital relationship. So, " '…the two – for one flesh;' this secret is great, and I speak in regard to Christ and to the assembly " (Ephesians 5:31-32). Remember when two or three gather in Christ's authority, He is in the midst (Matthew 8:20). God is working with believers to make binding decisions. Married believers hold this advantage, as well. The scripture, Deuteronomy 18:16, shows us that two or three witnesses establish something. Mankind or Adam is male and female (Genesis 5:2). God intends for us to be in unity and to use this union powerfully (Luke 22). So, God creates men and women, from the beginning, as equals. As Christians, we must marry fellow believers, see the God in our spouses and relish His presence.

When one mistreats a husband, a wife, a fellow believer that person also mistreats the God in him or her. Jesus warns that abuse is something He punishes. Also, Matthew 18:6 indicates it would be better for someone to bind a weight around the neck and throw him or herself in the deep, deep sea, rather than to stumble or to offend younger ones who humble themselves before God. Certainly, standing by without taking measures to protect someone is condoning the mistreatment. What would Jesus do? He would intercede and say, " Let her alone…" (Mark 14:16).

So, one could ask, "Where is God when such and such happens?" Well, I have an answer. Why isn't someone warning that person? Who or what prevents the criminal from serving jail time? Why is an individual unpunished after victimizing another? The answer is not to place blame with God, but to fix our broken system and change the laws to protect people from harm. We must be proactive and less afraid to speak up. We have to take responsibility and not be weary in well doing, because God gives us strength as we do His will.

One may ask: What is the purpose of God? Isn't He 'All Powerful'? The purpose of God is to be. He is all sustaining, always has been and always will be. He is the beginning and the end, the Alpha and the Omega. He never changes. What is meant for evil, God turns to good (Romans 8:28). Suffering loss may very well be the experience we dread the most. To suffer loss of a loved one, a limb, an opportunity, so forth, very likely may leave us with a feeling of betrayal or devastation. Consequently, if we allow God to turn a situation around, as hard as it may be, we will experience peace. The devastation people's evil actions cause cannot stop the power of God to heal and save souls.

So, doesn't God care? Yes, He does. You may ask, "Why has He let this happen to me?" I don't know. What about forgiving? Forgive, as you want forgiveness. That is how God will judge you. As you have forgiven others, He will forgive you. Almighty God, our Creator knows our hearts. Our focus should be on living holy lives and helping others to do the same. "Let all bitterness, and wrath, and anger, and clamour, and evil-speaking [blasphemy], be put away from you with all malice, and become one to another kind, tender-hearted, forgiving one another, according as also God in Christ did forgive you" (Ephesians 4:31-32).

What about rape? God's law commanded the death of the man who raped a betrothed woman (Deuteronomy 22:25). David's children came face to face with the horror of rape. According to II Samuel 13, Absalom conspired to kill his brother Amnon for raping Tamar, their sister. As promised by Nathan, David's house always had violence.

Regardless of how we felt about the situation, there were always consequences for sin. God extended his hand of mercy and grace, but He also destroyed. Evident in Jesus' response to the Pharisees, He rebuked them harshly for their hypocrisy. Jesus said, " ' He that is hating me, doth also hate my Father' " (John 15:23). To Jesus they were dead spiritually; whitewashed sepulchers, full of dead men's bones, liars who were to die in their sin and the devil for their father (Matthew 23:27; John 8:21, 24, 44). Unable to have the benefit of sleeping or dying like Lazarus and Jairus' daughter, to live again, these men were Hell bound.

Why allow hatred in your heart to grow for someone who is spiritually dead and facing judgment? This rancor of bitterness will only overtake your life. Why finish the wicked job started with evil intentions?

Forgiveness is necessary to render the attacker powerless, to relieve the burden of blame and to give control to the offended.

When Jesus endured betrayal, ridicule, brutality, crucifixion, and public humiliation; think about the people He died to save. The list included: the tax collector, the shepherds, the woman caught in adultery, a wayward son, a cheating husband, the thief on the cross, you and me. Christ extended forgiveness to us paired with responsible action to heal wounds of any size. Positioned to receive the gift of Christ has forced eternity to wait. Grace enabled us to have forgiveness rather than face God's wrath. Don't throw away God's love, while waiting to see what will happen. Christ has overcome the world (John 16:33). He has given you a choice to live for Him. God's gift was wrapped and placed in the tomb. What if you took Jesus' hand of friendship and asked Him into your heart? Take heed to the words of Joshua and his resolve, spoken to the Israelites: " ' And now, fear ye Jehovah, and serve Him, in perfection and in truth, and turn aside the gods which your fathers served beyond the River, and in Egypt, and serve ye Jehovah; and if wrong in your eyes to serve Jehovah—chose for you today whom ye do serve;--whether the gods whom your fathers served, which are beyond the River, or the gods of the Amorite in whose land ye are dwelling; and I and my house – we serve Jehovah' " (Joshua 24:14-15).

Everyone is made in God's image with the power to make decisions individually (Genesis 1:26-30). The choices one makes must include life. Jesus' power of the Holy Spirit gives life to raise the dead and dwells in every believer (Romans 8:11). Jesus is the Way, the Truth and the Life (John 14:6). Imagine dying without Christ and going to the final judgment of God, only to hear your deeds and go into the fire of Hell. That would be terrible for a person to wait an entire lifetime of curiosity; to face the chastisement and torment Jesus wants to take away, now.

It is for this reason that Satan is so instrumental in redefining marriage, manhood, womanhood and Godly living. Now, more so than ever, sexual boundaries are being erased. Too often, we want our way, ignoring God and still endeavoring to go to Heaven. Regrettably, many refuse to see removing Christ from the equation is a deception and prerequisite for an unfavorable reward. A masterful deception forged by Satan. This serves to reshape God's criteria for righteousness and creates an illusion reducing the power of God; giving rise to one that conforms to worthless standards. That form of blasphemy and idolatry is described in Romans chapter 1, along with the consequences.

Turning the attention away from the Lord pits the fight against righteousness, and with God. Obviously, God has the upper hand. Unfortunately, in the unrepentant sinner, the confusion and distraction this creates allows sin to rule. A society without morality is devoid of God. Perpetuating the lie that we may serve Christ through behavior the Bible clearly defines as sinful speaks to the erroneous perception of God and lack of humility. Thus the Church and its tenets now teeter over the abyss.

Marriage reflects God's relationship with His body, the Church. What better way to offend God than to redefine marriage, His establishment? The abomination of men lying with other men and reprobate individuals who find solace in behavior God deems shameful leads one to ask many questions (Leviticus 22:11; Romans 1:26).

As mentioned earlier, I asked God how to address the issue of sexual sin, when many people have been hurt and crushed through abuse. My desire was to avoid inflicting any more pain. I have found that many people engaging in sexually immoral lifestyles have been hurt through similar behavior. The very thing that caused the problem became the lure. God responded, " It is better to comfort with the truth, than to pacify with a lie."

Choosing values that shape the culture in which we live serve to confine or to liberate us as a nation. I have come to the conclusion that people have the right to be united to whomever they so choose. However, marriage reflects our relationship with God. Christianity pivots on this core value concerning the union of a woman with a man. Sex outside of marriage (one man and one woman) is whoredom. This behavior of unmarried persons living together and/or engaging in sexual relations, both heterosexual and homosexual, endangers their souls to experience the eternal second death or Hell.

For Christians and other believers, we must maintain the right to protect the Biblical teachings concerning marriage. Since Adam, God blesses marriage as a union between a man and a woman. Ignoring the perspectives of God carries a heavy penalty. By removing His provision and inheritance, one accepts a lesser and immediate gratification, which continues to jeopardize the eternal gift of salvation. Imposing values on believers that contradict the core foundations of our faith is bullying.

Today, many are choosing to become idolaters, fornicators, adulterers, sorcerers, liars and murders. If unrepentant, God will deny them entry into His kingdom, forever. Thankfully, there is hope and that Hope is Christ (I Timothy 1:1). So, as believers, we must no longer walk in the vanity of our minds, walking in ignorance outside of the life in God and the instruction of the truth found in Jesus (Ephesians 4:7-21). In our weakness we are made perfect in His strength (II Corinthians 12:9). It's time to be the salt of the earth, to stop cowering under the guise of falsehood. In effect, this behavior is concealing the true nature of righteousness and pretending that unrighteousness is acceptable through compromise. Rather, we should visit the widow, the sick, the fatherless, the orphan and the imprisoned being holy as God's children. I Peter 1:13-16 guides believers to be holy: "Wherefore having girded up the loins of your mind, being sober, hope perfectly upon the grace that is being brought to you in the revelation of Jesus Christ, as obedient children, not fashioning yourselves to the former desires in your ignorance, but according as He who did call you [is] holy, ye also, become holy in all behaviour, because it hath been written, 'Become ye holy, because I am holy' ". As for pure religion, James states, " If any one doth think to be religious among you, not bridling his tongue, but deceiving his heart, of this one vain [is] the religion; religion pure and undefiled with the God and Father is this, to look after orphans and widows in their tribulation – unspotted to keep himself from the world" (James 1:26-27).

Misunderstood Scriptures Deny Faith

When Martha's brother died, Jesus said, " 'Lazarus our friend hath fallen asleep, but I go on that I may awake him' " (John 11:11). Also, Jesus said Lazarus had died (John 11:14). Similarly, when Jairus' daughter died, Jesus also described her death as sleep (Mark 5:39). In the spirit realm, Jesus raised Lazarus from the dead. This authority that Jesus possessed over life and death was described in the Gospel of John. He said, " ' I am the rising again, and the life; he who is believing in me, even if he may die, shall live; and every one who is living and believing in me shall not die – to the age…' " (John 11:25-26).

In the New Testament account concerning Abraham, Lazarus (the beggar) and the rich man (Luke 16:23), all three men: Abraham, Lazarus and the rich man were physically dead. Unlike the rich man, who was in Hades and tormented, Lazarus found comfort in the bosom of Abraham. Just like John, loved by Jesus, rested on Jesus' chest.

How were these accounts connected? Well, Lazarus (Martha's brother) was sleeping, as were Jairus' daughter, Abraham and Lazarus (the beggar). Lazarus (Martha's brother), Jairus' daughter, Abraham and Lazarus (the beggar) were dead or sleeping. As my daughter, Candace, said once, "They haven't made it to their final spot." To Jesus these individuals had not been eternally damned like the rich man. How do we know this? Well, Jesus commanded Lazarus to come out of the tomb. Also, He called the spirit of Jairus' daughter to return to her body. Later, Jesus released himself from among the dead, then the souls of the departed, and their bodies from the tombs.

Even though the events of Lazarus in the tomb were unknown, what happened to a soul at death was described in Luke 16:23, 26. Abraham and Lazarus, the beggar, saw the rich man suffering in Hades, across the abyss. Neither were they able to reach the rich man, nor offer him any help. As recorded in Romans 6:23, the wages of sin is death; therefore, Christ's death, on the cross, satisfied the physical death required. Also, He became the first fruits from the dead as the first soul to rise after His sacrificial death. In addition, He was the first and only offering worthy to cleanse the soul and the spirit to rise from the dead. "And now, Christ has risen out of the dead--the first fruits of those sleeping he became" (II Corinthians 15:20).

Unfortunately, the rich man and others being tormented were unable to go to Paradise or Heaven. Mentioned earlier, the souls of Jairus' daughter or Lazarus, the brother of Martha and Mary, died and lived again. Jesus described the experience of Lazarus as sleeping (John 11:11). Yes, Lazarus was dead, but he and others could not have been the first fruits from the dead. Only Christ was able to suffer for our sins on the cross. Christ alone was the worthy sacrifice to be the first fruits.

As Jesus died, He released His Spirit from His body. As the messenger or angel at the tomb indicated, Jesus did in fact die. Speaking to the women, the messenger said, " '.... he is not here, for he rose, as he said; come, see the place where the Lord was lying; and having gone quickly, say ye to his disciples, that he rose from the dead; and lo, he doth go before you to Galilee, there ye shall see him; lo, I have told you' " (Matthew 28:6-7). The messenger or angel said Jesus died, rose and came out of the tomb. As the first fruits Jesus' soul rose, first. Then, God, the Holy Spirit gave Jesus life physically (John 6:63).

Jesus already became sin (II Corinthians 5:21) and died. That sin was not His, but ours. The only death Jesus experienced was physical. In Hades and separated from the God the Father, and the Spirit, Jesus used the power He was given. By His sovereign nature or self-empowerment, Jesus raised Himself from among the dead to release His soul. Jesus told his disciples at Galilee, " 'Given to me was all authority in heaven and on earth....' " (Matthew 28:18). (For additional verses about self-empowerment see: John 10:17-18; II Corinthians 5:21 and http:// biblesuite.com/greek/266.htm).

Unlike Jairus' daughter or Lazarus, Jesus took the full penalty for our sin: "for the wages of the sin [is] death, and the gift of God [is] life age-during in Christ Jesus our Lord" (Romans 6:23). Even though, He became sin, Jesus was self-originated or self-empowering. Expressing Himself apart from His Father, Jesus still respected His Father's will. Remember Jesus was sinless and God's promise in Psalm 15:2-5 obligated the Father to keep Him secure from slipping or being moved.

Jesus knew He was going to be separated from His Father and wanted this cup to pass. Had Jesus remained with His Father, we would have been lost to sin for eternity. In order for salvation to be available, Jesus had to be apart from His Father. This was the will of the Father and Jesus' dilemma. In my opinion, Jesus wanted to die for us, but agonized in the Garden of Gethsemane over His separation from His Father and the shame of sin, which indicated failure. Becoming the sacrifice for sin, Jesus was to be severed from His Father. If the Father had remained with the Son, Jesus would not have experienced death and resurrection alone as a man, nullifying the sole sacrifice of Christ, the Lamb of God, slain and worthy to open the scrolls (Revelation 5:6, 9).

In the Garden of Gethsemane Jesus conferred with His Father and sought His will. To signify His obedience and love for His Father and for us, Jesus said, " '...not my will, but Thine be done' " (Luke 22:42). Finally, on the cross, Jesus faced what he dreaded. After Jesus' separation from His Father, He cried, " 'My God, my God, why didst Thou forsake me?' " (Matthew 27:46). Offering Himself under the shadow of death, Jesus died. Later, the Father put an end to His Son's agony (Acts 2:24).

Just as a child grows into adulthood and learns to function apart from his or her parents, the maturation of Jesus' purpose occurs after His separation from His Father. Acting as the High Priest and sacrifice, Jesus dies on the cross to complete His work for sin and begins His descent among the dead alone. This brings to a conclusion all sacrifices for sin.

At death, Jesus preached to the souls in prison (I Peter 3:19) and asserted His authority over spiritual death. Upon His Soul's departure, Jesus also released souls from among the dead and opened the tombs. The deceased, whom Jesus freed, were seen in Jerusalem. Jesus executed the authority and power from the Father, having the keys to death and Hades (Revelation 1:18). Both to be thrown into the lake of fire along with those not written in the scroll of life (Revelation 20:14,15).

Experiencing his punishment across the abyss, the rich man had his reward of eternal punishment or death for sin (Romans 6:23). Christ's death satisfied this penalty for sin, as it related to the soul, body and spirit. So, only Jesus had the power to free the repentant sinner from eternal damnation. Jesus took this compulsory journey to Hades to signify His sovereignty as Lord and to exert His authority over death and life. God the Father loved Jesus, because He knew the Father and the Father knew Him. Jesus honored His Father and defeated the torment of the second death for all those believing in Him.

On the cross, Jesus said to the thief, " 'Verily I say to thee, To-day with me thou shalt be in the paradise' " (Luke 23:43). That day on the cross, Jesus assured the man that he would later join Him in paradise. Still on the cross and horribly marred (Isaiah 52:14), Christ took His last breath. He said, " 'It hath been finished' ". Jesus saw the upcoming fulfillment of: His work as the slain Lamb of God worthy to open the scroll (Revelation 5:9); the Redeemer who atoned for our sin (1 John 2:2; 4:10); the One who went into Hades (I Peter 3:19); He who fulfilled all things (Ephesians 4:10), the first fruits from the dead (I Corinthians 15:20); our risen Lord (Matthew 28:7; John 21:14; II Timothy 2:8). Conceivably, Jesus laughed as He later exited the tomb guarded by soldiers. To complete His final task, Jesus left in the same manner as His return, and ascended to heaven (Acts 1:11).

Maintaining His divinity Jesus' death also unifies the two flocks of believers (John 10:17-18). Only the Son's body dies to give the world life (John 6:51). Christ spiritually inhabits believers creating a new man (Ephesians 2:15; Ephesians 4:24; Colossians 3:10), and forms His temple (Ephesians 2:22). Corresponding to the Jewish temple, believers' bodies serve as God's sanctuary (I Corinthians 3:16). With three parts, the body represents the outer court; the soul is the inner court; and the holy of holies is the spirit. Jesus is speaking of Himself and says, " ' destroy this sanctuary, and in three days I will raise it up ' " (John 2:19).

Jesus' prophecy timeframe to rebuild the sanctuary coincided with the Hebrew lunar calendar. The days ended at sunset. God also changed the length of the days surrounding Christ's death. This was done previously by God as a sign, in Isaiah 38:8, to show Hezekiah's healing. Other occurrences were detailed in Matthew 24:22 and Mark 13:20. Before Jesus released His Spirit and died on the cross, there was darkness over the land: "And from the sixth hour darkness came over all the land unto the ninth hour" (Matthew 27:45). Jesus split Friday into two days. The darkness from noon to three o'clock was the first night of Jesus' death (a similar prophecy to Amos 8:9). After the daylight returned, this was the first day. When the Sabbath began that was the second night. The sunrise was the second day. On Saturday at nightfall, Sunday began. That was the third and final night. At sunrise, Sunday morning, on the third day, Jesus rose (Luke 23:55-24:3).

The sign of Jonah the prophet was three days and three nights in the belly of the fish. Jesus was three days and three nights in the heart of the earth (Matthew 12:39-40). Jesus rebuilt Himself, the temple, accordingly. The presence of God left the temple, and ripped the veil. About the ninth hour, Jesus released His Spirit into His Father's care. Jesus died, just as prophesied and declared (Isaiah 53:12; Luke 23:45-46). First, His soul was raised, then, the souls of the saints from Hades (I Peter 3:19), with their bodies out of the tombs (Ephesians 4:9). This was the first night for Jesus in the earth. When the sunlight returned, prior to the Sabbath, Jesus' body was placed in the tomb. This was first day for His body in the earth. When night fell again, the Sabbath began and this was the second night for Jesus in the earth. The Sabbath day was the second day. On the third night, when the Sabbath ended, Jesus' body was still in the earth or tomb. At sunrise, on day three, the Holy Spirit entered the tomb. So, Jesus fulfilled the prophecy and He rose on the third day. This signifies that life entered His body, then and not sooner. The Spirit departed at His death on the cross, and reentered His body in the tomb. Life of the soul was already in Jesus; therefore, only His body was dead. Sunday morning, the third day, was the resurrection of our Lord.

Unbeknown to the Pharisees and Chief Priests, prior to the Sabbath, Jesus had completed His work for our sin. Being first to die for our sin, Jesus also secured the right to be first over everything (Colossians 1:18). After the atonement for sin had been made, Jesus was the first to rise from the dead. Although Jesus raised Lazarus (John 11:25-27), Himself from the lower parts of the earth (Ephesians 4:9), and His soul from among the dead (Matthew 27:53), Jesus was the first soul raised after the sacrifice for sin was made. From reading the scripture, one may safely conclude that Jesus' soul went into the earth or tombs among the dead bodies, and the dead in Hades on the first night. Prior to the start of the Sabbath, and still daylight, His body was placed in the earth or tomb that evening. Last, when His Spirit entered His body and He rose from the tomb, on the third day, this completed the three days and three nights in the earth. Being the Word of God, at death, Jesus was able to divide soul and spirit (Hebrews 4:12). As God and man, Jesus possessed the authority over life and death. Having this authority, Jesus released the dead in Hades and revived the dead bodies in the tombs.

When Jesus released His Spirit the earth quaked, the rocks split and the tombs opened. Matthew recorded the event, "And Jesus having again cried with a great voice, yielded the spirit; and lo, the veil of the sanctuary was rent in two from top unto bottom, and the earth did quake, and the rocks were rent, and the tombs were opened, and many bodies of the saints who have fallen asleep, arose" (Matthew 27:50-52). Documented in Luke 23:44, the temple veil ripped and Jesus yielded the Spirit. Perhaps both accounts pointed to the sudden and simultaneous occurrence of the ripped veil and the released Spirit.

It was the sixth hour, when Pilate sent Jesus to be crucified; darkness was over the land (John 19:14-15). Jesus' shed blood and work for the forgiveness of sin began in the garden, continued throughout His scourging, and finally ended on the cross that first night. To elaborate, on the first night, Jesus' soul descended into the earth, and into Hades among the dead. Upon Jesus' death, many witnesses saw the dead in the holy city who were raised (Matthew 27:50-53). So, after Christ died, His soul rose first, and then He released those saints who were sleeping or dead. On the Sabbath, no activity by God was mentioned. Certainly, God rested according to His Word to keep the Sabbath holy. The third day, the Spirit entered Jesus and His body rose from the dead. This life has been given to us, as well (Romans 8:11; John 11:25). So, Jesus' Soul and His body along with the Holy Spirit were in the earth.

In the evening, before the Sabbath, Joseph of Arimathea requested Jesus' body from Pilate. After receiving Jesus' body, he and Nicodemus, wrapped Jesus in clean linen with 100 pounds of a mixture of myrrh and aloes and placed Him in a newly hewn tomb. This was the second day that Jesus was in the earth and the first day for His body. This also occurred before the Sabbath (Matthew 27:57-60; Mark 15:42-47; Luke 23:54; John 19:39-42). Mary Magdalene and Mary of Joses witnessed where Jesus was laid (Mark 15:47).

The Sabbath and the day after the preparation, with the third day approaching, the Chief Priests and the Pharisees wanted to prevent anyone from confirming Jesus' prophecy. So, they met with Pilate and asserted that Jesus' disciples would steal His body in the night and claim He rose from the dead, just as he said, on the third day. Hearing this Pilate dispatched a watch or guard (more than one soldier, according to Matthew 28:11) and told them to go away and make the tomb secure (Matthew 27:62-66).

On the third day, while it was still dark, Mary Magdalene went to the tomb (John 20:1). The other Mary went, also (Matthew 28:1). When the women arrived, an angel had rolled back the stone and was sitting on top of it. He announced that Christ's body was raised from the dead, and told the women to go and tell the disciples (Matthew 28:1-7). Sunrise had begun and the women just missed finding Jesus in the sepulcher (Mark 16:1-2).

We see the Father leads us to the Son, and through the righteousness Christ provides, a sinner may stand in the Father's presence. God's word is clear; " 'I am the way, and the truth, and the life, no one doth come unto the Father, if not through me; and from this time ye have known Him, and have seen Him' " (John 6:14). Christ enters Hades, because the souls need to see and believe in Him. Jesus says, " '…and this is the will of Him who sent me, that every one who is beholding the Son, and is believing in him, may have life age-during, and I will raise him up in the last day' " (John 6:40).

Since Jesus lived without sin, He was alive spiritually. Through Christ's triumph over death, every person was given the opportunity to experience the same victory over physical and spiritual death or *thanatos*. So, the life that Jesus gave on the cross satisfied the payment due for sin. Unlike the animal sacrifices continuously used to purify the flesh (Hebrews 9:13), Jesus' ultimate sacrifice paid the debt once, and in full required to remove sin. Reigning supremely, Jesus released the captives in Hades, after himself, to defeat spiritual death, and then, revived the bodies in the tombs.

As the Sabbath was approaching, Jesus fulfilled the whole law for our sin and freed the souls of the saints. Hanged on a tree, Jesus was cursed (Deuteronomy 21:23; Galatians 3:13), yet He delivered us from a life of bondage to sin and torment in Hell. Suffering shame, now glorified and resurrected, Jesus severed death's hold forever and "...led captive captivity..." (Ephesians 4:8).

Jesus had to die for our sins, because animal sacrifices were inadequate to redeem and liberate the souls of human beings from Hades. Animal sacrifices were unable to prevent the human body, soul and spirit from confinement in Hades, torment across the abyss, and the lake of the fire or second death. Consequently, Christ's sacrifice was unlike the deaths of Lazarus and Jairus' daughter. After His sacrifice, Jesus was the first to leave Hades on His own accord from among the dead.

With Christ's redemption, God overlooked sin (Romans 3:25). Once this change occurred, sinners were expected to reform (Acts 17:30). Forgiveness of sin has been available all along, and God has called or will call us all, at some point in time. Jesus' love for us sent Him to the cross and to Hades for the souls there. Nothing blocked salvation from the living or the dead.

In fact there are no barriers separating us from God's love (Romans 8:38-39). All have the choice to know the Father while living. Our Heavenly Father lovingly leads every soul to His Son (John 6:44, 65). All those who love the Father, eventually love the Son. God communicates with each person individually through his or her human spirit. These provisions from God offer all souls a way to avoid Hell.

In Revelation 20, at the great white throne after the scrolls and the scroll of life were opened, the dead standing before God were judged (vv.11-12). People who were dead came out of the sea, the death and the hades (v.13). Any names not written in the book of the life were judged for their works and cast into the lake of the fire, along with the death and the hades (v. 15). Condemned, they suffered the second death or second *thanatos*. The Greek word *thanatos* was "physical or spiritual death; (figuratively) separation from the life (salvation) of God forever by dying without first experiencing *death to self* to receive His gift of salvation" (2288 from Strong's Concordance, http: // biblehub.com /greek/2288.htm).

Jesus saves us from having to pay the debt of sin, "for the wages of the sin [is] death (*thanatos*)..." (Romans 6:23). Eventually, the final judgment sentences all: "And I saw a great white throne, and Him who is sitting upon it, from whose face the earth and the heaven did flee away, and place was not found for them; and I saw the dead, small and great, standing before God, and scrolls were opened, and another scroll was opened, which is that of the life, and the dead were judged out of the things written in the scrolls — according to their works; and the sea did give up those dead in it, and the death and the hades did give up the dead in them, and they were judged, each one according to their works; and the death and the hades were cast to the lake of the fire — this [is] the second death; and if any one was not found written in the scroll of the life, he was cast to the lake of the fire" (Revelation 20:11-15).

Women

All believers are to serve in quietness (I Timothy 2:2). Unfortunately, many use the scripture, I Timothy 2:12, to keep women from serving God and/or hamper their efforts to seek and to fulfill God's purpose. Let us examine the passage, I Timothy 2:12:

"and a woman I do not suffer to teach [to act as oneself], nor to rule a husband, but to be in quietness."

See: http://biblehub.com/lexicon/1_timothy/2-12.htm

On the surface this scripture seems very restrictive, but only forbids women from taking their husband's Godly authority and acting alone when instructing them. Jezebel comes to mind. This position also belongs to Jesus who does the will of the Father (Luke 22:42). So, wives must have a reasonable demeanor working with the husbands to accomplish the will of the Father. To say that women may not teach men is false. Mothers teach their sons and females teach males on every level.

As believers, instructing one another in the Lord is necessary and gender plays a role, as God designates. In the case of I Timothy 2:12, a husband has to be under God's rule. God forbids a wife to assert her knowledge, rule, and instruction over what God establishes for him. Only God has the authority to rule the development of a husband as the head of the wife. In like manner, Christ is the head of the Church, and gives himself for her.

Jesus, at the Garden of Gethsemane, set the example for husbands to follow. Before he gave Himself for us, His Bride, and died on the cross, He submitted to the will of His Father and not His own. God showed us how a husband, in earnest prayer, must prepare for his bride. This is a tall order and only God's authority and power may achieve such a feat. Driving a wedge between God and the husband is usurping the authority of the husband and being an obstacle to him. For a wife to interfere with the instructions God gives the husband is a mistake.

God has order and just as Samuel directed Saul, a wife must have an attitude of stillness and calm when working with her husband. Just as Jesus intercedes for us, husbands must go before the Lord. As Timothy said, the role of wife is not to usurp the authority of the husband. God deems this sacrificial service necessary for the wives' benefit, in order to make them spotless and without wrinkle. Therefore, Jesus was the example for husbands to follow and He alone must govern the husband as his head. So, Timothy is forbidding wives, out of their own authority, to teach husbands their roles. He is not restricting wives and/or women from teaching husbands and/or men.

Women hold other roles, as well. Like Jesus, believers, both male and female, have roles as kings and priests (Revelation 1:6; 5:10) and the right to share liberally the fruit of the Spirit (Galatians 5:22-23). Since the Levites would oversee the temple and the Law of the Old Covenant, a different priesthood is necessary for the new laws of God that Jesus issues. So, Jesus being in the order of Melchizedek, a king and a priest, oversees the New Covenant of God (Psalm 110:4; Hebrews 7:1, 21).

Jesus, spiritual husband to the Church, instructs believers. The husband, in turn, as the man in the house must receive instruction from God. The wife must receive instruction from God, as well. In fact, a believing wife and her devotion to God will allow an unbelieving husband to be useful to God or holy/hallowed. The same applies to the believing husband with an unbelieving wife (I Corinthians 7:14). Believers guide their spouses into a relationship with God. This devotion to God must be voluntary and compel the other to receive God's instruction. A wife shaping her husband, rather than God, illuminates the problem Timothy addresses. Husbands who spend time with God to learn how a man is to be a husband is the point of I Timothy 2:12. A wife must have faith, in her quietness, while God teaches her husband how to be a husband. If the husband refuses to submit to God, then God will deal with him accordingly and may give the wife leave of him as God has for me.

In a marriage, God is the boss over the husband and the wife. The scripture, I Timothy 2:12, in no way restricts women from serving as pastors, teachers or any other calling of God. Wives are simply restricted from usurping the authority God has given to their husbands.

The wife is obligated to follow God's will, not her husband's. Also, the husband is to follow God's will, not his own, nor his wife's. With one agenda, both the husband and the wife will experience the success of God's power as a unified force to do the will of God.

In the Bible, women held positions of leadership. Deborah was a judge of Israel and a prophetess who gave the king inspired instructions directly from God. The duties for a judge carried the weight and authority of Almighty God. Who, male or female, denied her authority because she was a woman? No one stood against God and won (Judges 4:4-8). Just as God guided Deborah to instruct King Barak, the Church needed to be taught by the authority of God (John 14:26). For God's purpose, He revealed and maintained our callings (Romans 11:29). So, despite her gender, God gave Deborah authority over men and women.

Ephesians 5:21 tells believers to submit to each other. Since there is neither male nor female in Christ, men and women hold equal authority as vessels of God. As one Church, Jew or non-Jew, we are one family and the apple of God's eyes (Zechariah 2:8). It is the authority of God in each believer that we should respect and obey.

The Holy Spirit filling a believer and giving him or her spiritual gifts is not limited by gender. We see, " ' The harvest indeed [is] abundant, but the workmen few; beseech ye therefore the Lord of the harvest, that he may put forth workmen to His harvest' " (Matthew 9:37-38). God forbid if women cease pastoral duties, teaching, preaching, evangelizing, helping and prophesying, etc. in the Church. God's Word, prophecy in particular, warns and instructs His children. Do we ignore the prophets' warnings simply because the instructions come from a women? How unfortunate for God to tell a woman to prophesy while others silence her? These traditions withhold the will of God by hindering women. In fact, to interfere with the message of a prophet brings about destruction from God (Isaiah 30:10; Amos 7:16-17).

In Revelation 1:6, God calls His people, both male and female, kings and priests, because Christ is a King and a Priest. Christ anoints the ones He chooses. All who accept Christ have the Living God with the power of a priestly king dwelling inside them. God wants His bride, the

Church, to be washed and holy without spot or wrinkle (Ephesians 5:27). He sees one body with neither male nor female (Galatians 3:6). Since gender holds no limitation for God, neither should it for us.

It's time to stop quenching the fire of the Holy Spirit (I Thessalonians 5:19) and flow with a river that runs deep. Souls need the well of compassion from Christ with His redemptive power. By working toward God's purpose, believers have the unlimited means to accomplish His perfect plan. The resulting bond is for God's glory. Therefore, inhibiting anyone in the family of God from fulfilling her or his designation is tantamount to sin and carries a high price.

Prayer

One morning the Lord woke me up specifically to pray for my sister. I asked the Lord what she was doing and He just took me in the spirit. Jesus held my hand as we started descending into a very dark place. I was so afraid to look anywhere except straight ahead, because there were things swirling all around us. God reassured me and said not to fear. After traveling a while, I knew that it was time. I also knew that my sister was in this dark place. So, suddenly, I closed my eyes, thrust out my hand, grabbed and pulled. Just then, Jesus and I left the darkness and I knew my sister was safe. Later, my sister told me that she knew when I prayed for her. That gave me an eerie feeling. So, we must intercede for one another, just as God intercedes for us (Romans 8:26, 34; Hebrews 7:25; James 5:16).

Retention of the Word of God comes with understanding. Matthew 13:19-23 explains in more detail. "Every one hearing the word of the reign, and not understanding – the evil one doth come, and doth catch that which hath been sown in his heart; this is that sown by the way" (Matthew 13:19). Aforementioned, to become a believer in Jesus Christ, we must fully receive the word of God, thus acting upon His Word, becoming doers and not hearers only: "and become ye doers of the word and not hearers only, deceiving yourselves, because, if any one is a hearer of the word and not a doer, this one hath been like to a man viewing his natural face in a mirror, for he did view himself, and hath gone away, and immediately he did forget of what kind he was; and he who did look into the perfect law – that of liberty, and did continue there, the one – not a forgetful hearer becoming, but a doer of work – this one shall be happy in his doing" (James 2:22-25). So, after receiving salvation, we must be doers of the word by working to please God and by giving an accurate meaning of the word of God. "...be diligent to present thyself approved to God – a workman irreproachable, rightly dividing the word of the truth" (II Timothy 2:15).

We must pray for one another following God's example. The "...Spirit Himself doth make intercession for us with groanings unutterable, and He who is searching the hearts hath known what [is] the mind of the

Spirit, because according to God he doth intercede for saints" (Romans 8:26, 27). All believers have the right to follow their calling and expect the protection afforded to them by God. God gives a specific warning: "Come not against Mine anointed ones, And against My prophets do not evil" (I Chronicles 16:22). David understands and heeds God's warning, as he spares Saul's life, God's anointed (I Samuel 19:23, 24; I Samuel 26:9).

Teaching

Jesus taught through word and deed. He used either the hammer of a fist, figuratively, or reached out with a helping hand of compassion. This proven example and 'hand of correction' teaching method has helped to guide the believer to judge righteously (John 7:24). Jesus hammered the Pharisees for their deception and manipulation. As a result of their objection to the righteous works of the Spirit through Jesus, He condemned them: " 'Ye are of a father -- the devil, and the desires of your father ye will to do; he was a man-slayer from the beginning, and in the truth he hath not stood, because there is no truth in him; when one may speak the falsehood, of his own he speaketh, because he is a liar -- also his father" (John 8:44). Conversely, Jesus, in a softer approach toward the woman at the well, asked her to bring her husband. Sparing her from humiliation, Jesus knew that she had five husbands, and was unlawfully united with her current husband. Jesus saw her as a sinner who needed His Living water to fulfill her unsatisfied desires (John 4:10).

In another instance, the Pharisees accused Jesus of casting out demons by the power of " 'Beelzeboul, ruler of the demons' " (Matthew 12:24). Jesus countered by insisting that forces divided could not stand. Also, He asked, " 'And if I, by Beelzeboul, do cast out demons, your sons – by whom do they cast out?' " Jesus went on to inform them that because of their actions, their sons would be their judges (Matthew 12:27). Similar sentiments were echoed in Revelation 5:9 and 10. John wrote about the coming kings and priests of God placed in the positions to reign on the earth.

Further, Jesus' warning stood then and now. Anyone who was not with Him was against Him, and anyone who was not gathering with Him was scattering. He made it very clear that "all sin and evil speaking shall be forgiven to men, but the evil speaking of the Spirit shall not be forgiven to men" (Matthew 12:31). For this reason, Jesus warned the Pharisees to believe the works, but instead they committed the unforgivable sin and blasphemed or spoke evil of the Spirit of God's work. Liberally, Jesus established forgiveness for the repentant sinner, not the evil, hardhearted one who spoke falsely of the Spirit of God

THE CONSCIENCE OF GOD

(Matthew 12:31-36).

In fact, Jesus exhibited disdain for the maleficent Pharisees who blasphemed the Holy Spirit, and then sought a sign. After a number of the Pharisees denied Jesus' power, these 'brood of vipers' (Matthew 12:34) had the nerve to ask Jesus for a sign. To which Jesus answered, " 'A generation evil and adulterous, doth seek a sign, and a sign shall not be given unto it, except the sign of Jonah the prophet....' " (Matthew 12:39). This group was not evil for seeking a sign. They were condemned for denying the holy power of the Spirit in Jesus to declare it the works of Beelzeboul. To call the miracles of Jesus by the Spirit of God the works of Satan, the Pharisees treated the Spirit of God with contempt and refused to acknowledge God's authority and works. They blasphemed the Holy Spirit, which in turn made them unrighteous and unfit for Godly service.

The birth of Christ was a sign. During the rule of King Ahaz of Judah, a plot to overthrow his kingdom was certain and God intervened. God told Isaiah to instruct Ahaz, the king of Judah, to petition Him. When Ahaz refused to obey God's request, God declared that He was sending a sign. Isaiah said, " Therefore the Lord Himself giveth to you a sign, Lo, the Virgin is conceiving, And is bringing forth a son, And hath called his name Immanuel, Butter and honey he doth eat, When he knoweth to refuse evil, and to fix on good. For before the youth doth know To refuse evil, and to fix on good..." (Isaiah 7:14-16). Then, God announced their future, "...Forsaken is the land thou art vexed with, because of her two kings" (Isaiah 7:16).

My study of God's pedagogy reveals these simple traits: demonstration, illustration, reason, command and revelation. God's grace, mercy and love demonstrate how to be delivered from foolishness (Proverbs 6:5). With parables, He paints pictures for us to learn about His wisdom (Proverbs 7:4-27). As we see in John 4:1-26, Jesus reasons with the woman at the well, and reveals that He is the Messiah they have been waiting to come and the Christ. With the rulers of Sodom and the people of Gomorrah, Jesus counsels them to turn away from sin (Isaiah 1:15-18). Today, as before, God tells us that He is one and commands us to love Him with our heart, soul, mind, strength, and to love others as ourselves. Through revelation, he shows us how He will circumcise the heart that one may love Him with all the heart and soul

TEACHING

to live (Deuteronomy 30:6; Mark 12:29-30).

Previously found in Exodus, the grave consequences for hindering God's children were vividly illustrated. Pharaoh's unbridled disobedience to God and unwillingness to submit to God's command to release His children brought tremendous suffering in Egypt. Ultimately, the death of the first-born of both people and animals, forced the king to allow the sons of Israel to leave. Hearing that the sons of Israel had fled (Exodus 14:5), Pharaoh pursued, like Saul who chased David, unrelentingly (Exodus 14:1,4,10). As the sons of Israel were escaping through the parted sea, Pharaoh's army followed. God through the pillar of fire and a cloud brought confusion to the Egyptian soldiers. Also, Pharaoh's chariots became stuck and were difficult to maneuver. When the Egyptian soldiers realized that God, Jehovah, was fighting against them, it was too late to flee. While the children of God were still crossing, God commanded Moses to stretch out his hand. The waters closed on Pharaoh's forces, killing every one of them, and their bodies washed up on the shore (Exodus 14:23-30; Psalm 136:15).

The sovereign Lord's standards are set. Instrumentally, God through revelation changes the heart from stone to flesh and puts His Spirit in the believer (Ezekiel 11:19; 36:26). Also, showing aspects of God's character, He uses dreams and prophecies to prepare those receptive to heed His warnings and willing to endure hardships for His glory. Both Joseph and John the Revelator come to mind. Matthew 13 also recounts Jesus' tool of parables to fulfill prophecy for those refusing to see, that hearing they eventually understand God's Word.

God enables believers to minister to the body of Christ: "and He gave some [as] apostles, and some [as] prophets, and some [as] proclaimers of good news, and some [as] shepherds and teachers, unto the perfecting of the saints, for a work of ministry, for a building up of the body of the Christ, till we may all come to the unity of the faith and of the recognition of the Son of God, to a perfect man, to a measure of stature of the fulness of the Christ, that we may no more be babes, tossed and borne about by every wind of the teaching, in the sleight of men, in craftiness, unto the artifice of leading astray, and, being true in love, we may increase to Him [in] all things, who is the head – the Christ" (Ephesians 4:11-16).

All of the ministries of the Old Testament that existed among the Jewish people were made available to those believing in Jesus Christ. He gave us designations for the purpose of equipping believers for the service of building the body of Christ. Christ, a perfect man, completed the will of the Father as an example for us to follow. He selected believers to perform tasks used to build and to grow His children as mature servants, serving one another for God's glory.

We must teach the fear of God. As one body of Christ, Jewish and non-Jewish believers exist, and it is a false notion to replace the Jews. Keep in mind, that 144,000 Jews, 12,000 from each tribe, the first-fruit to God, will walk the earth singing only a song they will be able to learn. In Revelation 14:3-4, these Jewish men do not defile themselves with women, and experience the protection of God's power. Further, God chastises Pergamos and Thyatira for teaching the church to eat idol food sacrifices and to practice sexual immorality (Revelation 2:14). To the church of Philadelphia, God condemns those falsely calling themselves Jews. So, the Jews in the church of God are distinct and pivotal in the final days on the earth before Jesus returns.

From examples given in Isaiah and throughout the scriptures (Jeremiah 44:30; Joshua 2:10), God warned, persuaded and eventually removed people as well as whole nations for rebellion. To reject the desires of God and continually sin resulted in iniquity. As seen in Saul's life, he was anointed and prophesied with the prophets of God. Tragically, he died in battle along with his sons for being unfaithful. Rather than consulting the Lord, he sought an audience with the deceased prophet Samuel and consorted with a witch to conjure his spirit (1 Chronicles 10:13). Being God's anointed; I pray Saul only lost his life and not his soul.

Having a more faithful end, Peter, once rebuked by Jesus (Mark 8:33), was converted and turned to become a great servant of God. In Luke 22:32, Jesus told Peter " '…and I besought for thee, that thy faith may not fail; and thou, when thou didst turn, strengthen thy brethren.' " Certainly Jesus expected His prayer for Peter to be answered.

The character of God, shown throughout the Bible, depicted a warlike, yet loving God. A vocal God, who listened, instructed, comforted, encouraged and prophesied. As Believers, God has commissioned us to emulate His example. Being made in the image of God, God expressly created us with three parts to resemble the Jewish temple, to have a body, a spirit and a soul (I Thessalonians 5:23). As the temple, our body was formed to represent the outer court; our soul to represent the inner court; and our spirit to represent the holy of holies. Some years ago, I shared this information. Later, I heard a preacher delivering this same information in her sermon. I'm glad God has spread His teaching.

God works by giving the message and confirming it in others. He always performs His good works for us and often through us. God's faithful character allows believers and non-believers to prosper under His guiding hand (Matthew 5:45). Before I became a Christian, God protected me and helped me through many hard times. Once on a school trip, after a hard climb up Mt. Kilimanjaro, I went to lie down on my bunk. To stay warm, I zipped myself all the way up in my sleeping bag. As I slept, I woke up realizing that I was struggling to breathe. The zipper of the sleeping bag was stuck and I was trapped in a lying position. Simultaneously, my sister came up the stairs to check on me asking if I wanted some cocoa. Squeaking out her name, I called, "Charmaine". Knowing that I needed help, I heard her run back down stairs yelling that something was wrong with Andrea.

Drifting off to a dark place, I died. I saw the room and was above everything, below. Then, everything went black and I saw a distant waving light. Something was telling me to stay away. With the darkness around me, I felt compelled to approach it. Ignoring the warning and moving closer to the light, I began to think that I should have listened. Just before I reached the light, I felt myself back in my sleeping bag. Someone had violently slammed me on the back, pushed me up and was screaming at me to breathe.

From what I remembered, she was one of the wives of a teacher who happened to be a nurse. Feeling tremendous stabbing sensations ripping my lungs, I said it hurts. The woman said I know it hurts, but you have to breathe. Growing up a tomboy, I was embarrassed when I began to cry. The woman told me to fan myself and I noticed that she slept in the bunk near me. Most of the night, Charmaine asked me if I was all right. How God loved me and blessed me with my sister. Thankfully, I lived to love Him and her.

No matter how wretched a soul may be, God waits patiently to bless. He gives us our lives as an opportunity to recognize Him and love others. He allows us to exist and gives us children as gifts to bless us. Always being a Father to the fatherless and a provider, God's character reveals His conscience to know what is right and to do it. Let us follow the example God establishes to know the truth, to be free and to be unique.

Having the liberty in Christ teaches us that our uniqueness is a gift from God. Shielded from a cyclical, self-imposed journey like the one Siddhartha takes, God's love nurtures and guides the believer to perform deliberate actions with fruitful results. Hermann Hesse, the author of Siddhartha (the book's title and main character), writes about a young man, who journeys far, only to find that his travels leave him empty and still questioning his identity. Siddhartha is unable to achieve his goal to find himself. This is not to be the case for a believer, or anyone for that matter. There is no need to find out "who you are", only to do what God requests of you, because you are special for great things (I Peter 2:9). Continuing to reject Christ, whom God places in Zion as a Rock, becomes a stumbling block to unbelievers. Just like the fictitious character Siddhartha lacks resolution at the end of his journey, so will unbelievers stumble over the Christ, when they disobey Him and try to walk in their own way (I Peter 2:8).

Apostle Paul's writings in Romans 8:28, teach "… to those loving God all things do work together for good, to those who are called according to purpose…" To hinder believers and our call of God "tribulation, or distress, or persecution, or famine, or nakedness, or peril, or sword…" (Romans 8:35) and all assortments of trouble come. Fear not, "but in all these we more than conquer, through him who loved us…"(Romans 8:37). To God we do "more than conquer", because conquerors often, if not always, lose part or all of their acquisitions. Through Christ abiding in each of us and each one abiding in Him, we win once and for all, securing a final and eternal victory. By allowing Him to use our unique gifts, for our righteousness, we must in turn remember that faith comes from God and be steadfast to complete our Godly assignments. Since God stands willing to accept us, we now know that we have the choice to receive Him as our Salvation. Refusing to be covetous, being content with the present things hear Jesus' words: " 'No, I will not leave, no, nor forsake thee' "

(Hebrews 13:5).

God also revealed to me why many saints continued to sin after they received Christ as their personal Lord and Savior. Many Christians/believers lived actively destructive and sinful lives, as Peter, because they needed to be converted. Jesus told Peter he had to turn (Luke 22:32). Peter had acknowledged Jesus as the Christ and Jesus confirmed that the Father had told this to Peter (Matthew 15:17). So, how did a man in whom the Father revealed this truth deny Jesus? The answer lies in the heart and will of a person to give himself or herself over totally to God, fearing God more than man. Following the Word of God, which is Jesus, requires refusing to manifest the works of the flesh: "adultery [fornication, idolatry, incest, (pornography comes from this word)], whoredom, uncleanness [impurity (the quality) physically or morally], lasciviousness [filthy, wantonness, lewdness, outrageous conduct, conduct shocking to public decency, a wanton violence], idolatry [image worship, worship or service of an image], witchcraft [the use of medicine for sorcery, drugs or spells], hatred, strife, emulations [zeal, jealousy with evil intent or malice], wraths [outbursts of anger, fierceness, indignation, passion as if breathing hard], rivalries, dissensions [standing apart, disunion, sedition], sects [a choice, (specifically) a party or (abstractly) disunion, heresy], envyings [ill-will (as detraction), jealousy, spite], murders, drunkennesses [intoxication], revellings [a carousal (as if letting loose), rioting], and such like…" Paul warned, "of which I tell you before, and I also said before, that those doing such things the reign of God shall not inherit" (Galatians 5:19, 20, 21). References come from an online source, which uses definitions from the Strong's Concordance: http:// biblelexicon.org/galatians/5-20.htm

Instead, let us manifest the fruit of the Spirit: "love, joy, peace, longsuffering, kindness, goodness, faith, meekness, temperance" (Galatians 5:22, 23). Also, in Galatians 5:25, 26, Paul tells the saints, "…those who are Christ's, the flesh did crucify with the affections, and the desires: if we may live in the Spirit, in the Spirit also we may walk; let us not become vain-glorious – one another provoking, one another envying!"

God teaches believers to turn away from all appearances of evil (I Thessalonians 5:22). This includes any thing that denies Jesus, substitutes the power of God or claims to be equal with God. Believers must put away reliance and belief in the power of horoscopes, astrology, palm reading, tealeaf reading, card reading or any other sources of power outside of Jehovah, God Almighty, Yeshua, Elohim, Jesus, the Holy Spirit, and other names for the God of the Bible.

II Timothy 4:2, urges the following: "to preach the word, be earnest in season, and out of season, convict, rebuke, exhort, in all long-suffering and teaching". Paul tells Timothy, every scripture is "God-breathed, and profitable for teaching, for conviction, for setting aright, for instruction that [is] in righteousness, that the man of God may be fitted – for every good work having been completed" (II Timothy 3:16-17).

Temptation

"The Lord hath known to rescue pious ones out of temptation, and unrighteous ones to a day of judgment, being punished, to keep" (II Peter 2:9).

James 1:14, "and each one is tempted, by his own desires being led away and enticed"

Matthew 4:1, "Then Jesus was led up to the wilderness by the Spirit, to be tempted by the Devil"

James chapter 1, verse 14, from my experience, is generally taught as one continuous thought. In fact, when evaluated the temptation of Jesus in the wilderness is not one, but two separate parts. Each one is tempted. That is a correct statement. The Spirit led Jesus to be tempted. It was God's desire for Jesus to endure temptation, as a human experience, and to ready Jesus for His role as the High Priest (Hebrews 2:17). The seed of Abraham, not angels, were subject to the fear of death and bondage (Hebrews 2:15). Since all who believe are Abraham's seed and blessed with him (Galatians 3:7), believers know that Jesus freed us from the bondage of death as the high priest and sacrificed himself for our sin (Hebrews 2:16-17). Jesus became a human being and died to defeat the devil's power over death (Hebrews 2:14). Also, Jesus delivered people from the fear of death and bondage (Hebrews 2:15). Additionally, Jesus became flesh to perform the duties of the high priest (Hebrews 2:17). Last, Jesus, as a person, experienced temptation to help those who were also tempted (Hebrews 2:18).

Clinging to his waning power, Satan tempted Jesus in James 1:13. God led Jesus, but Satan tempted Him. Satan foolishly desired to keep Jesus from being the sacrifice and provision to cancel sin. Due to the fact that God's righteousness required punishment for sin, in Matthew chapter 4, Satan's goal was to force humankind into eternal damnation without a way of salvation. Attempting to circumvent Jesus' holy sacrificial offering, as the worthy lamb, Satan tried to prevent anyone from reigning with Christ. To blemish the sacrifice of God would have resulted in the rejection of the offering. Without a substitute for Jesus, we all would have been dead in our sins, heading for certain spiritual death and eternal Hell.

Jesus certainly was led by the Spirit, not led away nor enticed, because He knew all of humanity would have been damned forever without His sacrifice. Becoming the curse and hanged on a tree, Jesus took the punishment for our sin and bought our freedom from Hell (Galatians 3:13). Experiencing life and death, our sinless Lord Jesus transformed life and death to secure His position as the lamb of God, the only one worthy to open the scroll with the seven seals (Revelation 5:9). Jesus had to die to bear much seed. He said, " '…verily, verily, I say to you, if the grain of the wheat, having fallen to the earth, may not die, itself remaineth alone; and if it may die, it doth bear much fruit….' " Without Jesus' resurrection breaking the power of death, the prophecies would have been nullified, the souls with Abraham trapped and the names written in the Book of Life deleted (Revelation 20:12-14).

As seen earlier, Jesus was tempted in the wilderness, but He did not yield to the temptation, nor did Jesus want to do evil. Having the authority of God, Jesus resisted the Devil, taught with finality and lived without sin. Led by the Spirit, Christ was not drawn away by His own desires and enticed. It is evident in the scripture that Jesus continually pleased His Father (Matthew 3:17; Matthew 17:5; Mark 1:11; Luke 3:22; II Peter 1:17). He also used His creative power in the restoration of sight to the blind, showing the evidence of Jesus as the Creator and the Word. Manifesting the power of God in the flesh, Jesus became the promise of salvation. God's faithful promise produced descendants for Abraham and the culmination of Christ our Savior. Ultimately, God swore by the highest authority, Himself. "For to Abraham God, having made promise, seeing He was able to swear by no greater, did swear by Himself" (Hebrews 6:13).

With His commandments, the Lord endeavors to keep His children from going astray and makes armor available for our protection. While the Old Testament laws illuminate sin, the New Testament writers introduce removal of sin through Christ. Believers are able to stand against the Devil's deceit, by putting on the whole armor of God (Ephesians 6:11). The sword of the Spirit is the Word of God and must be wielded with great accuracy. So much so that when questioned about the first of all commandments, Lord Jesus reminded the Scribes not only of the oneness of God, but loving each other. "Hear, O Israel, the Lord is our God, the Lord is one; and thou shalt love the Lord thy God out of all thy heart, and out of all thy soul, and out of all thine understanding, and out of all thy strength – this [is] the first command; and the second [is] like [it], this, Thou shalt love thy neighbour as thyself; – greater than these there is no other command' " (Mark 12:29-31).

When Satan seeks to hinder God's children by posing confusing interpretations of God's instructions with ambiguous standards, it is too difficult to judge right from wrong. An example of this tactic may be seen in Genesis. In an attempt to undermine God's will, the devil asked a misleading question. The serpent's question contained a lie. To confuse Eve to misremember God's instructions, the serpent asked her whether God had forbidden them to eat of the trees of the garden. God directs Adam, male and female, not to eat of the tree of the knowledge of good and evil, only. The plan worked, because Eve told God that she had forgotten (Genesis 3:13).

Satan posed the question to allure Eve. By tempting Eve, Satan became a stumbling block to her. Once Eve decided that the fruit of the tree of the knowledge of good and evil was good to eat, she forgot God's instruction. With the desire formed, along with the deceitful prodding, Eve and Adam ate the forbidden fruit. Consequently, Adam attempted to absolve himself by blaming Eve. Although they were both led away by their desires and enticed, their desires did not cause them to be tempted. Just as Satan tempted them, he also tempted Jesus. Their choices were to be led by God or by their desires and enticed. Similarly, God told Cain in Genesis 4:7, " '…Is there not, if thou dost well, acceptance? And if thou dost not well, at the opening a sin-offering is crouching, and unto thee its desire, and thou rulest over it' ".

God tempts no one (James 1:13). Those who change His truth into falsehood to serve creatures rather than the Creator, He turns over to the desires of their hearts (Romans 1:24-25). Their desires entice and led astray. Choosing not to acknowledge God, God relegates them to mental depravity without the capacity to reason. They know God by the visible evidence of His creation; yet choose to replace the incorruptible God with images of corruptible man and animals. The end result is considerable uncleanness in thought and deed: " all unrighteousness, whoredom, wickedness, covetousness, malice; full of envy, murder, strife, deceit, evil dispositions; whisperers, evil-speakers, God-haters, insulting, proud, boasters, inventors of evil things, disobedient to parents, unintelligent, faithless, without natural affection, implacable, unmerciful; who the righteous judgment of God having known – that those practicing such things are worthy of death – not only do them, but also have delight with those practicing them " (Romans 1:18-31).

We hold to God's teachings to govern our behavior and desires. God judges sin and we must read the Holy Bible knowing that eternal damnation is only God's to administer and to govern. Our actions are to reflect God's greatest commandment, to love Him with all of our heart, soul and mind (Matthew 22:37). His second great commandment is to love one another as we love ourselves. Let us speak the truth in love (Ephesians 4:15), live holy, righteous lives, turning from evil and encouraging others to do the same.

To be tempted means just that and nothing more. Jesus was tempted by the Devil (Matthew 4:1), but God is not tempted of evil (James 1:13). Evil doesn't affect God. Satan placed many choices before Jesus, who rejected the evil. In fact Jesus answered Satan with the Word of God, Himself, and resisted Satan until he left. Having been and continually being tempted by the Devil, when the Spirit leads us, we have God's power to resist the Devil and evil, as well.

We are tempted no matter what our desires are. If we succumb, we are led away by our desires and enticed. Our desires have no bearing on being tempted, only on being led away and enticed. This is why, when tempted, believers know that God is able to save them. Our armor protects us and the angels fight for us.

God has given the resources to handle temptations and live holy lives:

1) Fight with the Word:

> "But he answering said, 'It hath been written, Not upon bread alone doth man live, but upon every

word coming forth from the mouth of God.'" (Matthew 4:4)

2) Assemble with other believers:

> "not forsaking the assembling of ourselves together" (Hebrews 10:25)

3) Edify, build up each other, correct, encourage and support each other in the Lord:

> "So, then, the things of peace may we pursue, and the things of building up one another..." (Romans 15:2).

> "and we exhort you, brethren, admonish the disorderly, comfort the feeble-minded, support the infirm, be patient unto all" (1 Thessalonians 5:14).

4) Know those who work to lead you in the Lord and hold them in high esteem and be at peace:

> "....to know those labouring among you, and leading you in the Lord, and admonishing you, and to esteem them very abundantly in love, because of their work; be at peace among yourselves (1 Thessalonians 5:12-13).

5) Call upon the Lord and the angels for help:

> "For Thou, Lord, art good and forgiving. And abundant in kindness to all calling Thee" (Psalm 86:5).

> "are they not all spirits of service – for ministration being sent forth because of those about to inherit salvation?" (Hebrews 1:14)

6) Fasting and prayer to cast out demons:

> "…and this kind doth not go forth except in prayer and fasting'"(Matthew 17:21).

7) Know the Holy Scripture:

> "be diligent to present thyself approved to God -- a workman irreproachable, rightly dividing the word of the truth" (2 Timothy 2:15).

8) Live righteously, trusting in the Lord and His sacrifice:

> "not giving back evil for evil, or railing for railing, and on the contrary, blessing, having known that to this ye were called, that a blessing ye may inherit" (1 Peter 3:9).

In fact, other sacrifices used as substitutions for Christ were insufficient and worthless. The animal sacrifices of the Old Testament did not remove sin. We no longer needed the sacrificial animals, since we had been given something better, the blood of our Redeemer, Christ, Yeshua.

> "for by one offering he hath perfected to the end those sanctified" (Hebrews 10:14).

9) Control your thoughts:

> "As to the rest, brethren, as many things as are true, as many as are grave, as many as are righteous, as many as are pure, as many as are lovely, as many as are of good report, if any worthiness, and if any praise, these things think upon" (Philippians 4:8).

10) Let Christ lead you and give you the desires of your heart and run from sexual immorality:

> "flee sexual immorality" (I Corinthians 6:18).

> "for we were once -- also we -- thoughtless, disobedient, led astray, serving desires and pleasures manifold, in malice and envy living, odious -- hating one another; and when the kindness and the love to men of God our Saviour did appear (not by works that are in righteousness that we did but according to His kindness), He did save us, through a bathing of regeneration, and a renewing of the Holy Spirit, which He poured upon us richly, through Jesus Christ our Saviour, that having been declared righteous by His grace, heirs we may become according to the hope of life age-during" (Titus 3:3-7).

God's mercy

When God rained on the just and the unjust (Matthew 5:45), He extended mercy to all. This was evident in the story Jesus told of Lazarus, a poor man, and the rich man (Luke 16:19-31). Mercifully, God gave the rich man numerous occasions to show pity to Lazarus. Placed at the rich man's porch, even the dogs came to comfort Lazarus, and licked the sores covering his body. How Lazarus wished to eat just the crumbs from the rich man's table. Conversely, the wealthy man lived well. He was "making merry" daily and dressed elegantly (v. 19).

The mercy of God provided the option and the ability for the rich man to change his heart and the destitution of the poor man. Rather than showing kindness to Lazarus, the rich man relinquished any obligation, and instead focused on himself and his interests. God's mercy was shown to the rich man during his life and Lazarus at the end of his. Had the rich man acted to relieve Lazarus' unfortunate circumstances, he would have had a change of heart. Then, God would have had the foray to minister to his soul. Sufficed to say, at death angels took Lazarus to Abraham's bosom, and the rich man to damnation.

God ensured that the paths of Lazarus and the rich man crossed. Allowing the rich man with the opportunity to change the suffering of Lazarus showed God's mercy. Judged for his works, the selfish man was cast into the torment of Hades (v. 24). From there the rich man asked Abraham to send Lazarus to bring some water to quench his thirst. While alive, the rich man neglected to help Lazarus. Once dressed in elegant, dyed clothing, he ignored the suffering of Lazarus. Now, he wanted Abraham to send Lazarus to dip just his finger in water to comfort him. Not even suffering changed the rich man. He still refused to acknowledge the value of Lazarus, made in God's image, and expected him to be ordered to fetch some water.

In my own walk with God, He shows me how merciful He is to me. I could rationalize my wickedness to console a disquieted conscience, and toss in my spirit, only to find death in the end. Then, how could I face a pure and loving God, walking with boldness to His throne? By

His grace, He lets me live another day. Christ's death shows the mercy of God to take away my wickedness, giving me a way of escape from Hell for my sin. He waits extending a hand of forgiveness for you, as well. Take it.

How God loves us. He cares deeply for you and me. When God says in Matthew 7:23, "…depart from me ye who are working lawlessness", He is speaking of those who make a consistent effort to sin and continue in their sin, unashamed. Having the trappings of godliness and the heart of a serpent, those who are lawless conceal their true intentions by operating in a seemingly lawful manner. Deceiving others, these individuals appear godly, but inadvertently desire the glory belonging to God.

Similar problems were seen in Ezekiel chapter 21. When the Lord remembered the sins of Israel's children, they were to be slaughtered by the sword. "Therefore, thus said the Lord Jehovah: Because of your causing your iniquity to be remembered, In your transgressions being revealed, For your sins being seen, in all your doings, Because of your being remembered, By the hand ye are caught" (Ezekiel 21: 24). The Lord cut off both righteous and wicked children of Israel (Ezekiel 21: 3 and 4). Manifold were the sins of the children of Israel (Ezekiel 22). They were shedding blood (v.3); made idols for defilement (vv.3-4); near and far scoffed at them and they abound in trouble (v.5); honor for parents was gone (v.7); foreigners in the land were oppressed (v.7); fatherless and widows were oppressed (v.7); holy things were despised and the Sabbaths were polluted (v.8); men of slander were shedding blood (v.9); these men of slander were eating and dwelling together with the people (v.9); had sex with family members (vv.10-11); took a bribe to shed blood (v.12); interest or usury and increase were taken (v.12); cut off their neighbor through oppression (v.12); forgot God (v.12); dishonest gain and again for shed blood (v. 13). For these and other sins, God said, "The house of Israel hath been to Me for dross, All of them [are] brass, and tin, and lead, In the midst of a furnace – dross hath silver been…" (Ezekiel 22:18).

In the New Testament, God forgave sin, but punished the deceitful. There were those calling, "…Lord, lord, have we not in thy name prophesied? And in thy name cast out demons? And in thy name done many mighty things?" How shameful for them to think they fooled

God. He said, "...I will acknowledge to them, that – I never knew you, depart from me ye who are working lawlessness..." (Matthew 7:22-23). Although they appeared to be casting out demons, God was. Luke recorded, " but if by the finger of God I cast forth the demons, then come unawares upon you did the reign of God" (Luke 11:20).

From my personal experiences with demons, I know they manifest and withdraw to avoid expulsion. Only the power of God is able to remove them. That is why Jesus questions the Pharisees' doubt of the power by which He cast out demons. Professing that Jesus uses Satan's power to cast out the demons, Jesus is adamant about His position. He pronounces judgment on the Pharisees for their unwillingness to recognize God's power in Him. Consequently, He reverses the position of the child and the parent, positioning the sons to judge the men (Matthew 12:27).

Not only were the Pharisees and chief priests full of doubt, but fearful. Afraid the people would follow Jesus, because of His signs, the Sanhedrin consorted to kill Him (John 11:47, 53). Concerned that Jesus' acceptance would bring the attention of the Romans, they dreaded losing their land and people (John 11:48). Even the promise God made to David, to give Israel a land to inhabit (2 Samuel 7:10) and to Amos (Amos 9:14-15) was forgotten.

God mercifully sent his prophets to warn, to inform and to direct His anointed and others. For example, Saul, a valiant warrior and courageous king, ignored the Lord's commands. He fell as a result of his fear of the people. Regrettably, he lost his kingdom: "for a sin of divination is rebellion, and iniquity and teraphim [insubordination] is stubbornness; because thou hast rejected the word of Jehovah, He also doth reject thee from being king'" (1 Samuel 15:23).

Caiaphas, fortunately feared God, fulfilled his duties to the Lord and prophesied correctly. Caiaphas, the high priest, rebuked the Sanhedrim saying, " 'Ye have not known anything, nor reason that it is good for us that one man may die for the people, and not the whole nation perish.' And this he said not of himself, but being chief priest of that year, he did prophesy that Jesus was about to die for the nation, and not for the nation only, but that also the children of God, who have been scattered abroad, he may gather together into one" (Joel 3:2; Luke 11:49-52).

Through the scripture, we know no one is righteous, "Because there is not a righteous man on earth that doth good and sinneth not" (Ecclesiastes 7:20). However, the righteousness Christ affords us through His forgiveness is the fulfillment of the law. As believers, we are in Christ, "and of Him ye – ye are in Christ Jesus, who became to us from God wisdom, righteousness also, and sanctification and redemption" (I Corinthians 1:30). The law identifies sin (Acts 3:20), but does not bring about righteousness. So, we may only achieve holiness and right standing with God through faith in Christ (Romans 3:22). Also, "...if in the light we may walk, as He is in the light – we have fellowship one with another, and the blood of Jesus Christ His Son doth cleanse us from every sin" (I John 1:7). As we confess our sins, God is certain, through His righteousness, to forgive us and cleanse us of our sins and unrighteousness.

Glorifying God and refusing to take any credit for His work shows maturity in Christ and the death of selfish tendencies. This humility allows us as believers to recognize God's mercy and to bring His love into focus. Those observing our behavior, also have the opportunity to witness the reverend response to the Lord. Personally acknowledging one's sin gives Christ the permission to operate in the individual and opens his or her heart to fully experience forgiveness as God's mercy. Wiping away sin is available to the believer as we see in Acts: " '...to this one do all the prophets testify, that through his name every one that is believing in him doth receive remission of sins' " (Acts 10:43). Salvation comes individually. For those believing in Christ there is no difference (Romans 3:22). We are one family in Christ of Jewish and non-Jewish believers.

Although the Church is one body in Christ, His body has many parts with active Jewish customs. The Revelation of Jesus Christ, by John, clearly indicates that particular events, from Jewish traditions and culture, occur prior to Christ's return. Specifically, God protects 12,000 from each Jewish tribe during the Revelation tribulations and judgments (Revelation 7:5-8). God rebukes the church at Pergamos for "holding the teaching of Balaam, who did teach Balak to cast a stumbling-block before the sons of Israel, to eat idol-sacrifices and to commit whoredom" (Revelation 2:14). Finally, Christ's holy city, New Jerusalem, comes from heaven to the earth (Revelation 21:2), where God and the Lamb are the sanctuary or temple (Revelation 21:22).

Recently, God revealed other important teachings to me about unifying the body and working for the Lord to keep His body holy. They may be used to eliminate the bitterness, uncertainty and presumption felt by believers burned out in ministry. Jesus blessed us with standards to handle circumstances and to execute godly decisions to remove deception and the sale of wares in the house of worship. For instance, repeatedly, Jesus hammered the Pharisees for criticizing His healings and His good works. When the Pharisees attempted to kill Jesus and claimed Abraham as their father, He told them their father was the Devil (John 8:44). Also, He constructed a whip, drove the merchants out of the temple, released the animals being sold, poured out the coins of the money-changers, overthrew their tables and commanded those selling doves to take them out and not to make His Father's house a house of merchandise (John 2:13-17). See: Matthew 21:12; Mark 11:15-17; Luke 19:45-46. Yet, to the Samaritan woman at the well, Jesus asked her for a drink. Knowing the Jews did not associate with the Samaritans, she questioned Jesus. When Jesus described her life, she marveled and brought others to meet Him. Based on the woman's preaching many of the people believed that Jesus was the Christ (John 4).

Consistently, Jesus has given sinners opportunities to repent and to have a place with God, no longer burdened by the weight of sin. Jesus mercifully challenged the unbelievers in the temple. They doubted the Father was in Him and He in the Father. He urged them to at least believe His works, and then they would see the Father was in Him (John 10:38). This work of God's mercy afforded the unrepentant souls a way to freedom from sin. With His free gift of salvation, they had the option to repent and to receive a new life.

Love

While I was completing this book, the Lord told me to include a chapter on love. Very much a novice of the Greek language, I began studying the New Testament and learned new details about two verbs used in the Bible for love. For example, the verb *agapaó* and the noun form *agapé* referenced God's love. The verb *philéo*, and the adjective form *philos*, pertained to the love between friends. According to the HELPS ™ Word-studies *agapé* and *agapaó* or God's love had a moral commitment and preference or choice. To practice Godly love meant to do God's will. The references stated:

"**Cognate: 25** *agapáō* – properly, to *prefer*, to *love*; for the believer, *preferring to "live through Christ"* (1 Jn 4:9,10), i.e. embracing God's will (choosing His choices) and obeying them through His power. **25** (*agapáō*) preeminently refers to what *God prefers* as He "is love" (1 Jn 4:8,16). **See 26** (*agápē*)" (biblehub.com/greek/25.htm). "**26** *agápē* – properly, *love* which centers in moral *preference*. So too in secular ancient Greek, **26** (*agápē*) focuses on *preference*; likewise the verb form (**25** / *agapáō*) in antiquity meant "to *prefer*" (*TDNT*, 7). In the NT, **26** (*agápē*) typically refers to *divine love* (= what *God prefers*)" (http://biblehub.com/greek/26.htm).

Philéō and *philos* were described as follows: "**5368** *philéō* (from **5384** /*phílos*, "affectionate friendship") – properly, to show *warm affection* in intimate *friendship*, characterized by tender, heartfelt consideration and kinship" (http://biblehub.com/greek/5368.htm).

"**5384** *phílos* – a friend; someone *dearly* loved (prized) in a personal, intimate way; a trusted *confidant*, held dear in a close bond of personal affection. *Note*: The root (*phil-*) conveys *experiential, personal* affection – indicating **5384** (*phílos*) expresses *experience-based* love. [**25** (*agapáō*) focuses on *value-driven* (an [a] *decision-based*) love – which of course does not exclude affection!]" (http://biblehub.com/greek/5384.htm).

Both forms of love were used in John chapter 21. Here, a resurrected Jesus appeared to His disciples and provided them with a tremendous catch of fish. After they enjoyed their meal on the shore, Jesus asked Peter if he loved Him and used the word *agapas*. When Peter answered Jesus, he responded with a love from *philéo*. Twice Jesus asked Peter if he loved Him to do His will. Each time Peter said he loved Jesus as a friend, minus the commitment of Godly love. Jesus, then asked Peter if he loved Him as a friend. This instantly cut through Peter as he insisted to repeat his love for Christ as a mere friend.

Agapaó was used to prefer to love with a commitment like Jesus who sacrificed His life for us. He loved us, because He "is love" (1 John 4:8, 16). The verb form was used and not the noun. To me this indicated that the action of God *is* love. When Jesus asked Peter if he loved Him the word used for love came from the word agapé. This was a preference to love by doing the will of God. Jesus inquired if Peter loved Him enough to do His will. Peter responded that he loved Jesus as a friend, or *philéo*, each time. Finally, Jesus no longer asked Peter if he preferred to do His will, but instead if he had the love of a friend, only. Jesus used the word derived from *philéo*. To this Peter was grieved and told Jesus that He knew all things.

Examination of the scriptures showed me the all encompassing, unflinching love of God. The type that nothing and no one has stopped. So, without a doubt to love God required the power of God Himself. Believers equipped with God's love were given the authority to overcome the fear to follow God's will. Tasks assigned by God coupled with divine persuasion or faith allowed the believer to accomplish them. To have faith meant having God's assurance. If God promised to complete a goal, then that was certain. Thus faith gave birth to belief in God's promises.

A well-known promise made by God was recorded in Genesis 18. God appeared to Abraham among the oaks of Mamre. Abraham had been sitting at the opening of the tent. When Abraham looked up, he saw three men and rushed from his tent to meet them. He asked them to stay and to accept his hospitality. Abraham requested the servant and Sarah to quickly help him to prepare a meal for the guests.

Afterward, the men asked Abraham where Sarah, his wife, was. He told them that she was inside the tent. Then, one of the men prophesied that he would return by the same time next year and that Sarah was to have a son. Sarah heard and laughed to herself. She also questioned if she could have sexual pleasure in her old age and considered the advanced age of her husband, as well. Immediately, God knew that Sarah had laughed and included Abraham in the discourse. God questioned Abraham and asked why Sarah laughed and doubted that she was to bear a child in her elder years. God also asked, " '...Is any thing too wonderful for Jehovah?' " (Genesis 18:14). When Sarah was confronted, she denied that she had laughed, because she was afraid. Finally, it was established that she had indeed.

Focused on the inability of a woman to bear children past their reproductive years, Sarah's laughter signaled doubt about God's promise. Not only had she disbelieved the idea of motherhood, at her age, she brought God's ability into question. God spoke directly to Abraham concerning Sarah, and then to her. Regardless, as promised, Sarah had a son. He was named Isaac or the sound of laughter, perhaps as a reminder to Sarah of God's ability to fulfill His promises. God lovingly with swiftness corrected, forgave and showed His commitment to follow through with His promises. He loved Sarah and blessed her with what she thought was impossible.

Hence, the love God has for us is limitless. Without wavering, God shows us how to have His love residing in us. In I John, chapter 4, God details the steps necessary to know and to believe the love that He has for us. By perfecting the love residing in believers, God gives us the boldness to approach Him without fear in the Day of Judgment. Replacing the human will with that of God is only possible by His power. Our willingness to allow God to work through us takes supernatural strength. With His love and our submission, we are able to confess Jesus as the Son of God.

John writes, "whoever may confess that Jesus is the Son of God, God in him doth remain, and he in God; and we — we have known and believed the love, that God hath in us; God is love, and he who is remaining in the love, in God he doth remain, and God in him. In this made perfect hath been the love with us, that boldness we may have in the day of the judgment, because even as He is, we — we also are in this world; fear is not in the love, but the perfect love doth cast out the fear, because the fear hath punishment, and he who is fearing hath not been made perfect in the love; we — we love him, because He — He first loved us; if any one may say — 'I love God,' and his brother he may hate, a liar he is; for he who is not loving his brother whom he hath seen, God — whom he hath not seen — how is he able to love? and this [is] the command we have from Him, that he who is loving God, may also love his brother" (I John 4:15-21).

Circling back to the important conversation Jesus had with Peter showed the relevance of doing God's will. In order to love one another, God obligated believers to love as He did. Through Jesus' interaction with Peter, we saw the need to conform to the ways of God for the benefit of all. As a result, Peter's soul conversion took place when he reconciled his needs with God's will. In the end, Peter preferred God. This victory highlighted the need for every believer to die to self, in order to love like God.

Rapture Myth

The scripture Mark 4:23 says: " 'if any hath ears to hear – let him hear.' " In subsequent verses the emphasis is upon measuring someone by her or his own standard and adding to what she or he has. Hearing and receiving the seed or God's Word, along with producing a harvest depends on the condition of the heart. So, without planting the seed in one who hears, receives the Word in his/her heart and bears fruit, what little one has of God's Word is unfruitful.

Hearing was mentioned throughout the Bible. Jesus spoke to the seven churches: Ephesus, Smyrna, Pergamos, Thyatira, Sardis, Philadelphia, Laodicea. Every church had specific warnings with different rebukes; however, each time Jesus ended with these words: "He who is having an ear — let him hear what the Spirit saith to the assemblies" (Revelation 1:10). To the church of Smyrna, Jesus warned that they were going to have tribulation and to be tried by Satan. Jesus encouraged them not to fear, but instead to overcome, in order to receive the crown of life. For the Church at Pergamos, their downfall involved following the ways of Balaam, which taught the Jews to eat sacrifices to idols and to commit whoredom.

Lack of hearing the Word of God and disobeying, together, pose a great threat to God's people. Having a seared conscience, delusional persons fall away from the faith and champion others to follow them. They succumb to "seducing spirits and teachings of demons". These "hypocrites" forbid marrying and compel others to abstain from consuming food God deems suitable for human consumption with thanksgiving, sanctified by the word and intercession (See: I Timothy 4:1-3, and an earlier discussion concerning broma).

Adhering to God's instructions provides blessings found in the Bible, His Word and Son, Jesus Christ. Dull hearing, ignoring God, hardens the heart (Exodus 10:1; Mark 6:52; Luke 9:13). Sowing the Word by the way affords no chance of producing a harvest. An insufficient root system forms, when scattering the seed on the shallow or rocky ground, giving the birds an opportunity to eat the seed and the sun to wither it.

As children growing up my father would say us, "Your ears are hard of hearing", when hearing and ultimately disobeying. One who hears much will have more added, and one who hears little, even it will be taken away. " 'He, who has an ear to hear – let him hear.' " He who has much fruit and the word, more will be added. He who has little, even it will be taken away (Mark 4:9; Revelation 2:7). As Romans 10:17 states, "so then faith [is] by a report, and the report through a saying of God". Like little or wavering faith is unsustainable, so is little hearing and reception of the Word which is responsible for cultivating the fruit.

In terms of the first-fruit of God and the lamb, 144,000 virgin, Jewish men, remain after the slaughter of believers holding to their faith in Christ. Except for this remnant of men, all other believers apparently suffer complete eradication, since God judges all, except for the remnant (Revelation 6:9; 7:14; 14:1, 3, 4). This occurrence points to judgment of everyone on the earth, minus the remnant, and the imminent return of Jesus (Revelation 9:4; 14:1). Only the Father knows when Christ will return (Matthew 24:36), but thankfully, when the seventh trumpet blows, voices from Heaven will declare the kingdoms of the earth are the Lord's and His reign is forever (Revelation 11:15). At Christ's appearance, "...the Lord himself, in a shout, in the voice of a chief-messenger, and in the trump of God, shall come down from heaven, and the dead in Christ shall rise first (I Thessalonians 4:16). Jesus "...shall send his messengers with a great sound of a trumpet, and they shall gather together his chosen from the four winds, from the ends of the heavens unto the ends thereof" (Matthew 24:31). The dead in Christ are the first to rise, then those who are still living on the earth to meet Jesus in the air (I Thessalonians 4:16-17). It seems the only remaining believers left on the earth are the 144,000, who gather with Jesus on Mt. Zion (Revelation 14:1).

It is my sincere belief that the popular 'rapture' teaching deceives the Church to blindly embrace apostasy. From my understanding of this message, God takes up or raptures His children before His return and they escape the 'Great Tribulation' on the earth. If the rapture removes believers from man's violence, then the teaching is false. What I find in the Bible indicates much suffering for believers for aligning with Christ (Matthew 24:9; 24:21-22; 24:27; 24:29-31; John 15:18 to 16:4; Revelation 13:7). By refusing to languish in sin (Revelation 14:12-13; 16:6), believers are subject to torture and execution (Revelation 14:12-

13). God's children are slain, because of the word of God and for their testimony (Revelation 6:9). With their last breath, God's children are speaking of His goodness. The saints, wearing white robes at the throne, ask God to avenge their deaths (Revelation 6:10, 11). Before delivering another series of punishments to affect the land, sea or trees, God's four messengers seal the 144,000 Jewish men (Revelation 7:3-8; 14:1; 14:3-4).

As Jesus lives in glory, for His sacrifice and drinking the cup (John 18:11), His disciples and all believers will have the same cup to drink (Mark 10:39; I Corinthians 7:11-34). Gladly many remain in Christ and overcome. God says, happy are the saints who are dying, because they rest from their labors: "And I heard a voice out of the heaven saying to me, 'Write: Happy are the dead who in the Lord are dying from this time!' 'Yes, (saith the Spirit,) That they may rest from their labours — and their works do follow them!' " (Revelation 14:13). The intense purging of believers from the earth will leave only the 144,000, God's elect, alive to meet Christ in the air, after the dead in Christ go up, first.

Having been so pressed concerning this information, I wrote a letter, in 2007 to local pastors. On May 23, 2007, I also addressed the letter to Christians and posted it online. For the purposes and consistency of this book, the letter was revised to only include scripture references from the Young's Literal Translation of the Bible.

Dear Christians:

I am writing to you concerning teachings about Christ's return and the tribulation. It is a favorable assertion of many in the body of Christ that Christians will be 'raptured' prior to the tribulation. God has indicated to me that this teaching is deceiving His people. As a result, many will be unprepared for the hardships to come and blame God for their suffering. All too often, God is blamed for the acts of Christians and not what He has done.

The word of God is crystal clear about the return of Christ. The Revelation and I Thessalonians [I Thessalonians 4:16] record a loud voice and a trump upon the return of Christ. Specifically, Revelation 19 tells us the seventh trumpet will sound prior to Christ's return

[Clarification: Specifically, Revelation 19 tells us Christ returns. Prior to Jesus' return, the seventh messenger sounds in Revelation 11:15].

This reveals the order of Christ's return subsequent to the tribulation. Also, Matthew 24:8 and 21 indicate that there will be "sorrows" and a "great tribulation" before Christ's return. God will even shorten the days after the fourth messenger pours out his vial on the sun for the "chosen" (Revelation 16:8; Matthew 24:22). Mark 13:24-27, " 'But in those days, after that tribulation, the sun shall be darkened and the moon shall not give her light, (Revelation 16:10, the fifth messenger) and the stars of the heaven shall be falling, (Revelation 16:17-21, seventh messenger) and the powers that are in the heavens shall be shaken. " 'And then they shall see the Son of Man coming in clouds with much power and glory, and then he shall send his messengers, and gather together his chosen from the four winds, from the end of the earth unto the end of heaven' " (Mark 13:26-27).

So, Christ will return after the tribulation with the dead in Christ first, and then, the messengers will gather those on the earth. Paul, like John, explains " for if we believe that Jesus died and rose again, so also God those asleep through Jesus he will bring with him, for this to you we say in the word of the Lord, that we who are living – who do remain over to the presence of the Lord – may not precede those asleep, because the Lord himself, in a shout, in the voice of the chief-messenger and in the trump of God shall come down from heaven, and the dead in Christ shall rise first" (I Thessalonians 4:14-18).

Please consider changing your teaching to reflect the word of God. It is critical to teach the word of God with accuracy as we work out our salvation with "fear and trembling". My hope it that this letter will result in a modification of your views of Christ's return and the events as simply stated in the Gospels, I Thessalonians, and The Revelation of Jesus Christ.

Sincerely,

Andrea Russell

Regardless of our views pertaining to Christ's return, let us teach what the Word says. As we seek first God's kingdom and His righteousness, we welcome God's blessing and seek His face to shine upon us. " 'Jehovah bless thee and keep thee; Jehovah cause His face to shine upon thee, and favour thee; Jehovah lift up His countenance upon thee, and appoint for thee – peace. 'And they have put My name upon the sons of Israel, and I – I do bless them.' " (Numbers 6:24-27).

In Deuteronomy 6:4-5 the children of Israel were commanded to hear and to love God. " 'Hear, O Israel, Jehovah our God [is] one Jehovah; and thou hast loved Jehovah thy God with all thy heart, and with all thy soul, and with all thy might.' " The greatest command to Love God was passed to the next generations. Jesus reiterated this command in the New Testament. The directive was to love God with all your heart, soul, mind, strength and understanding (Matthew 22:37; Mark 12:30; Luke 10:27). Also, Jesus commanded the love of a neighbor and considered a neighbor to be someone in need (Luke 10:30-37).

By focusing on what the Lord desires, we love with our minds and bodies. To treat each other with the love of Christ is the key. Jesus gives us examples to follow, correcting lovingly, and reprimanding as He does. In Matthew 12:34 and Luke 3:7, He calls the Pharisees hypocrites, vipers, and such. Behavior that God deems unrighteous impacts others; therefore, warrants harsh criticism.

As believers, we have the honorable task of helping those in need, encouraging one another and spreading Christ's teaching of love. Via our actions, let the world see Christ bringing nonbelievers to faith rather than repelling them. The way we treat one another, whether agreeing or disagreeing, signifies the love in our hearts for Christ.

The fruit of the Spirit (Galatians 5:22-26) and the fruit of righteousness (Philippians 1:11), reflect a heart to serve God. Also see: II Corinthians 9:10. Godly love abounding to know and to judge things that are acceptable to God culminates the fruit of righteousness. Living beyond offense, blameless and without causing sin is only achieved through Christ.

The Bible implores the reader to avoid unholy living and requires all to follow God's commandments. Myriad pitfalls exist in this world, with dire consequences threatening the faith of a believer. Thankfully, abiding by the teachings of God offers security. Let us abandon the temporal and fleeting attractions before us that lead to death. Instead, we should look forward to the stability of a future eternity and wait with anticipation, to overcome, to meet God in Heaven, and to talk with our Creator with contentment to hear. The victory we have, as believers, now and forever is worth any sacrifice necessary to keep our names from being blotted out of the Lamb's book of life.

Revelation 2:11, "…He who is overcoming may not be injured of the second death."

Revelation 2:26, " '…he who is overcoming, and who is keeping unto the end my works, I will give to him authority over the nations…' "

Revelation 3:2, " 'He who is overcoming – I will make him a pillar in the sanctuary of my God, and without he may not go any more, and I will write upon him, the name of my God, and the name of the city of my God, the New Jerusalem, that doth come down out of the heaven from my God – also my new name.' "

Revelation 3:5, " 'He who is overcoming – this one – shall be arrayed in white garments, and I will not blot out his name from the scroll of the life, and I will confess his name before my Father, and before His messengers.' "

Revelation 3:21, " ' He who is overcoming – I will give to him to sit with me in my throne, as I also did overcome and did sit down with my Father in His throne.' "

My Testimony

While I was in high school, my Dad was contracted to teach at Egerton College in Kenya. My love for Africa began a few years earlier when we lived in Tanzania. Although I was born in Nigeria, we moved when I was eighteen months old and I was too young to appreciate the rich culture there. Having found out that Dad had taken a job in Kenya, I felt compelled to go, too. Something inside was drawing me.

In Kenya, the only secular American school we found stopped at the eighth grade. Continuing our search for an American high school, we found a missionary school. As an agnostic, I was so unhappy to attend a religious school and prepared myself to resist being influenced by doctrine. To my surprise, I met many wonderful people and made good friends. However, the infighting about religion was damaging to my perspectives of God.

At RVA, I became good friends with Kathleen Walberg. Consistently, she prompted me to seek the Lord. Unconvinced that God existed, this was not on my agenda. Her persistence sparked a curiosity for the unknown. So, I began to question if there was a higher power. Over a period of one and a half years, I requested any supreme being to reveal itself to me, if it existed. Slowly, my inclination faded and I stopped asking.

One day, on my way back to my dorm, I heard someone call my name. Naturally, I thought a friend of mine was calling me from the Algebra room and hiding. I said, "Jokes on me, ha ha, you got me". Then, I heard my name a second time. This got my attention, because I didn't see anyone. Finally, I heard my name in front of me and above my head. I froze. A tremendous fear came over me, since I was just joking around and laughing at the voice. From the base of my abdomen a feeling rose out of me and I heard myself answer, "Yes, Lord". I covered my mouth and contended that I hadn't given myself permission to speak.

Next, a butterfly flew up to my face and hovered there. I decided that if it was going to look at me, then I was going to look at it. The butterfly looked like a monarch. The insect was very beautiful with magnificent coloration, spindly legs that just dangled and lumps all over its head, or eyes. As I finished examining it, it seemed to know and flew away.

Once again the voice spoke and said, "Look to the left". When I did, I saw the flowers in bloom casting their colors in waves toward us. The voice said, "Look to the right" and the flowers were doing the same. As I looked to the left again, I saw two white butterflies or moths. I said if this is the God of the Bible it would be: Father, Son, Holy… Just as I began to say Holy Ghost, a third butterfly or moth joined the two. At this point I was deathly afraid, because I had doubted which God it was. Again the voice spoke to me and said, "Look all around". When I looked, I saw no one, not even a bird in the sky, neither a herder on the hill, nor a woman carrying firewood, nor any animals. It was just the two of us. Last, the voice said, "I have made all this".

Elated that I had received an answer, I seemed to float down the steps unaware of my movements, as I continued to my dorm. On the way, I ran into Serena Denmark. She said, "Andrea, what has happened to you?" All I did was smile. I was unable to talk and tried to pull my face in order to speak. With the smile still plastered on my face, I just shook my head and went into the dorm. My immediate thoughts were of Moses. He was the only person in the Bible I could remember with whom God spoke. I thought, wow, God actually spoke to me.

I wondered if the Bible was true and if Jesus was the Son of God. Soon, I began hearing words and long passages. I didn't know what they were. Also, I prayed out loud to God, the way I had as a child when I recited my standard bedtime prayer.

So, I questioned the voice and asked Him to tell me if the Bible was truly His word. Someone may have overheard and left a Bible on my bed. I began to read the Bible, but it was a paraphrase and I didn't find it to be authentic. I heard the voice tell me to go and buy a Bible. This particular week, I had drained my school bank account and only had 7-9 shillings or about $1.50 US left. I knew that wouldn't buy a Bible anywhere. The voice persisted and told me to go buy a Bible.

The following weekend, I went on the weekly school trip into Nairobi. Walking around I saw a plaza with a courtyard. I knew a bookstore had to be in the shopping center. As I suspected, there was a bookstore and I went inside. A carousel with Bibles displayed was in the middle of the store. As I perused through the Bibles, looking for the cheapest one, I came up empty and left. I heard the voice say go back into the store. As I returned to the store the clerk left the counter to help me. I opened my hand and showed him how much money I had. He simply looked at my money and kept searching through the books. We went from top to bottom, front to back and found nothing in my price range. I asked him if he had any more Bibles. He responded that he had placed all of the Bibles in the store on the carousel. Once again, I left the store. The voice said, "Go back". I said okay and turned around.

Entering the store for a third time the clerk met me at the carousel. This time there was a Bible for exactly what I had in my hand, right in front of us. I said this wasn't here when we looked. The clerk agreed. Another man came from the back room. He was trying to talk, but nothing came out of his mouth. Quickly, I tried to hand the clerk the money and take the Bible. Refusing to take the money there, the clerk insisted to complete the sale at the cash register. All along the other man was still at the carousel trying to talk. I turned my back to him and focused on the clerk. As soon as the clerk handed my Bible to me, I immediately left the store.

Now, back in my room, with a Bible in hand, I opened it only to see the passages that I had heard in my head. Frightened, I closed the Bible. After about a week, I went to read my Bible, again. I saw more passages that I had heard in my head. Scared, I decided to wait a longer period of time before reading the Bible. This time, I waited about a month, with the same result. Once I saw that the Bible was God's word, I then needed to know if Jesus was His Son. Knowing the Bible was God's word; I concluded that it must be true concerning Jesus. I wasn't sure what to do, but I remembered that others had asked Jesus into their hearts and for forgiveness. So, I knelt down beside my bed and began to pray. Remembering an experience from my childhood, when I had asked Satan to possess me to give me power, I cast two demons out of myself. I said time to go and said good-bye to the left and to the right.

When I was younger, I was baptized. Now, that I actually believed in

Jesus as my Savior, I asked to be baptized, again. At the time of my baptism, I remember all of my body went into the water, except the tip of my nose. I laughed thinking God had already done a little work in me that didn't need to be changed.

As a new Christian, I did my best to recite the Bible scripture that I selected for my baptism. The passage was from Jeremiah 10:10:

"And Jehovah [is] a God of truth, He [is] a living God, and a king age-during, From His wrath shake doth the earth, and nations endure not His indignation".

About the Author

Both of my parents were educators from Jamaica. Raised as a Jamaican citizen, I was born in Nigeria, West Africa, and became an American in 1999. Due to my father's work with the Jamaican and American governments, our family traveled extensively. After high school, I returned to the United States to attend college. Graduating with two degrees in Art Education, I worked as an art educator for fifteen years. With a heavy heart, I decided to leave teaching to live out another dream and started a graphic design business in 2002.

By the age of five, my mother had already taught me to read and to write. I learned mathematics from my father and knew how to multiply, before the third grade. From kindergarten to the third grade, I attended St. Norbert School in Winnipeg, Manitoba, Canada. I completed my primary grades at Bessemer Elementary School. Continuing my education in Greensboro, NC, I went Mendenhall Junior High School for my seventh grade school year. Moving to Tanzania, I attended the International School of Moshi (ISM). Back in Greensboro, I completed my freshman and sophomore years at Grimsley High School. My desire to return to Africa was so great, that I convinced my father, with my mother's assistance, to allow me to travel to Kenya where I graduated high school from Rift Valley Academy (RVA) in 1982.

Upon returning to the United States, I studied at Bennett College, also in Greensboro, from 1982-83, but transferred to East Carolina University (ECU) in Greenville, NC. There I received my BFA in 1987 and MAEd in 1990. From 1991 to 1994, I finished my coursework, but did not complete my PhD program at The Ohio State University.

During my studies at The Ohio State University I married, and then divorced my husband. Consequently, I was separated from my stepson, Elshaad. This broke my heart, because I had no legal standing as a guardian to raise him. Thank God, he found my daughter online. After over twenty years of separation, we had a fantastic reunion. Praise God.

Family ties and community involvement have always been important to me. My parents inspired me to serve in the community, which cultivated the sense of compassion that I have for others. In essence,

ABOUT THE AUTHOR

they gave birth to my desire for ministry and a responsibility to help those in need.

So, when I saw a man digging through our trashcan for food, I knew something had to be done. For a couple of days, at the same time, this man appeared in the alley. Noticing, I wrapped up a plate of hot scrambled eggs and toast and placed it on the trashcan. As I watched for him through the window, I saw that he examined the food, but did not eat it. Soon, I went to see if something was wrong with the food. Immediately, the Lord revealed to me that he didn't want to eat the food conspicuously placed there. God asked me if I would have eaten it. I admitted that I wouldn't have eaten food placed on a trashcan. The man only trusted what he found, even if it was in the trashcan, but not what someone left for him. On my way back to the house, I looked at our big garage. It was then that I knew this space needed to be used for ministry to help the homeless.

Retrospectively, I should have given the food to him personally. Over the years, God has taught me how to minister. The Lord has shown me to pray before approaching anyone and how to have a kind heart and a humble spirit. Expressing joy with a warm smile has opened the closed doors of people's hearts to me.

At about the same time that I had the inclination to use the garage to help the homeless, I discussed with my daughter about being the Church and not just going to church. On the way to worship, we passed so many people. In my mind, I kept wondering who was ministering to them. Once, we even walked to our worship service, just to pray for our neighbors. Every one we talked to reached out their hands and prayed with us.

Following the Lord's lead, we began our ministry. With my daughter's help, we started a prayer walk and created the acronym H.O.M.E. or Helping Others Maintain Equity. I designed business cards with our message, and God cautioned me not to print too many. Each Saturday night, I waited for the Lord to give me a direction for us to walk the next day. If I didn't get one, we knew to stay home. Sunday mornings or shortly after noon, regardless of the weather, we walked up and down our street and prayed for those we met. God even placed on the heart of one of our neighbors to be our intercessor. Di Benedetti (a.k.a. Matilde M. Tupas) prayed diligently for us.

During our walks, we saw one miraculous healing. A man had fallen off his bike and injured his arm. When I prayed for him the pain went away, but the swelling persisted. The Lord told me to ask my daughter to pray. She put her hand on me and I placed my hand on the man's arm. Once she prayed, in a few moments, the swelling went down. I told him to keep praying and to go see a doctor.

On the way back to the house, Roger, another neighbor, approached us for prayer. He reached out one hand and was trying to hide his cigarette behind his back with the other. I told him God wasn't worried about that and insisted that it was more important to pray. He immediately gave his life to the Lord. Afterward, he offered to fix us breakfast. My daughter declined, so I walked her home and returned. Having a chance to meet his girlfriend, I found out that she was a Christian. They were living together and Roger desperately wanted to marry her, but she was afraid. A failed relationship had left her scarred. I hoped our time together helped, because they have since moved. How grateful I was that Roger gave his life to the Lord.

Another Sunday, we helped a neighbor and prayed with several children who were preparing to start the school year. All of the children gave their lives to the Lord. A family friend who was there to take the children to buy school supplies helped to gather the children and assisted us.

We also helped our elderly neighbor to walk on her front porch. She continued to say that she didn't think she could do that, but she did. We asked her to change her words from can't to can. As we were leaving, we encouraged the daughter to continue to work with her mom.

Keith, our neighbor who lived on Weber Road, had skin cancer. He received prayer several times and acknowledged his faith in Jesus. Even with the cancer consuming him, he never complained. Each time we went to pray for him he was always peaceful and kind, sadly, he died. Thankfully, he went to be with the Lord in comfort.

We spoke with our neighbor who lived on the next block and let her know what we were doing. She said that she was Catholic and didn't normally talk to anyone, but welcomed us to stop by any time we were out walking.

On our last day, with one card left, we walked to a local store. I asked my daughter if she wanted to do the honors and hand out the remaining card. Both of us wanted to give the other the blessing. Finally, at the store, we encountered a man who was reluctant to talk with us. We assured him that we didn't want anything from him, but just wanted to tell him that he was valuable and had equity, like his home. After that he took the card. The card had the same message we shared with him. As he was reading it, we began to walk away. To avoid the perception of appearing overly zealous we walked toward the door. As we were leaving, the man began talking to us. Soon, he enthusiastically began sharing experiences about his life with us for quite some time. Before we parted, I asked him to consider Jesus as his God. He said he would and almost apologized for talking so much. We told him that we didn't mind and he seemed glad that we had met.

We began cleaning out the garage to help the homeless. Before our organization was established and organized, the Holy Spirit told me to open. One of our volunteers, Victoria, had been wonderful to help reduce the clutter and brought her grandchildren for fellowship. After dinner, she asked me how she could pray for me. I asked her to pray for people to come.

About 9:00 pm, just as I was closing the garage door, a man walked by and asked if he could cut the lawn, to make a little money. Since the job was promised to someone else, I offered him a meal, instead. As he ate, he told me that he was on his way to ask for an advance from one of his lawn service clients, so he could buy something to eat. God knew he was going to show up in need of a hot meal.

We solicit prayers for God's will and to set-up a non-profit. As the Spirit leads, please fast for us to continue serving others. In Jesus' Name, we also commit to pray for God's will to be done in the lives of fellow believers. We will also fast for the cause of Christ, rebuke all evil attacks, judge according to God's will, uphold righteousness and pray for those in need.

Dear Reader:

Thank you for purchasing, <u>The Conscience of God</u>. May God richly bless you. May His face shine upon you. May you forever be in His care.

God grant you His Love and Abundant Blessings, in Jesus' Name.

Sincerely,

Andrea L. Russell
Author

Notes:

The Conscience of God

Lunar Calendar

Friday

There was darkness the sixth to ninth hour / Noon to 3 pm (Matthew 27:45; Mark 15:33; Luke 23:44).
Jesus was still with Pilate the 6th hour (John 19:14).
About the ninth hour Jesus cried out twice and died (Matthew 27:46 and 50).

Friday was split into a second night and day:

Day One: Jesus' body was in the tomb.

Night One: Jesus' Soul went into the earth.

Created by Andrea L. Russell

The Conscience of God

Saturday

Lunar Calendar

On the Sabbath, Jesus' body was still in the tomb.

Night Two

Day Two

Created by Andrea L. Russell

The Conscience of God

Lunar Calendar

Sunday

Day Three: Resurrection Day - Jesus' Body was raised from the dead. "Jesus answered and said to them, 'Destroy this sanctuary, and in three days, I will raise it up'" (John 2:19). The additional night and day on Friday, fulfilled the prophecy of Jesus in the earth for three days and three nights (Matthew 12:40; 16:21).

Night Three

Day Three

Created by Andrea L. Russell

The Conscience of God

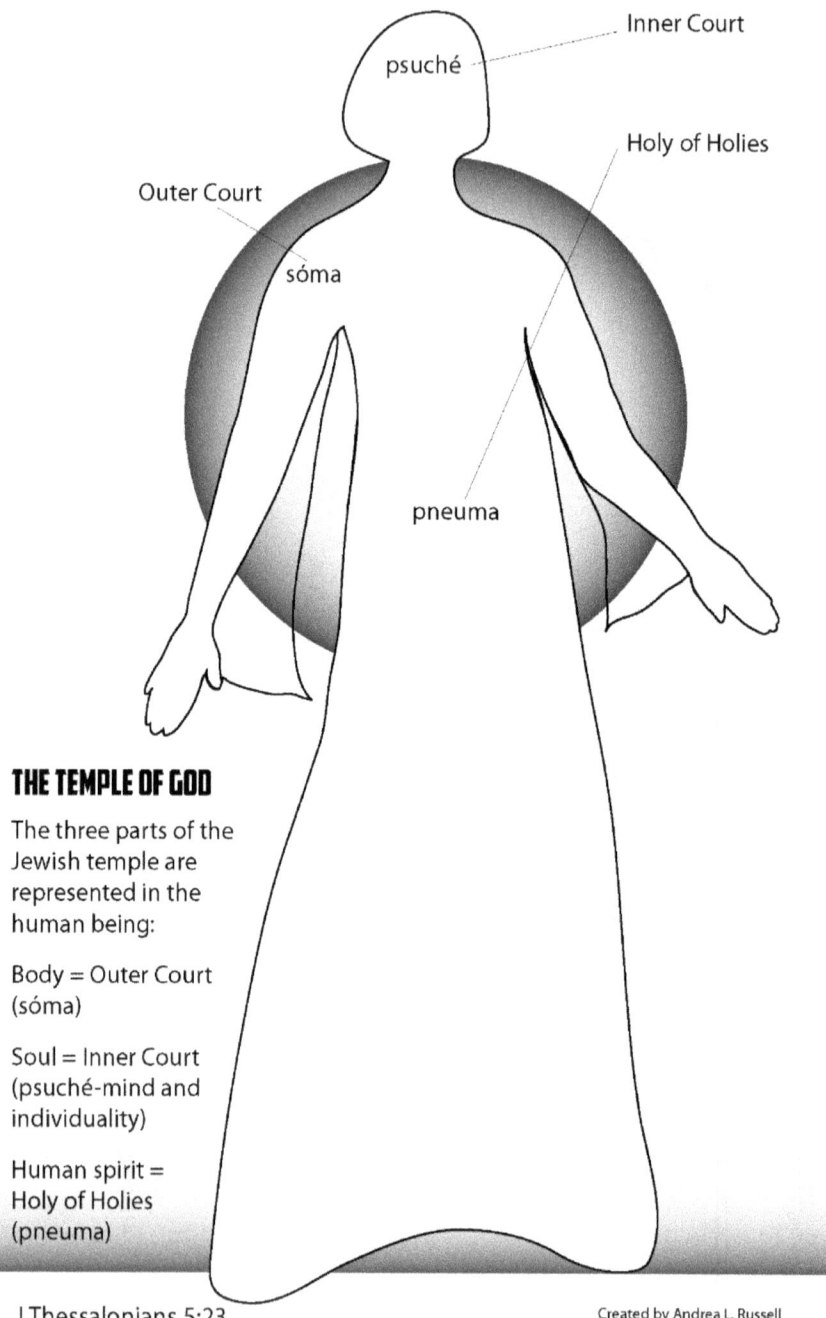

THE TEMPLE OF GOD

The three parts of the Jewish temple are represented in the human being:

Body = Outer Court (sóma)

Soul = Inner Court (psuché–mind and individuality)

Human spirit = Holy of Holies (pneuma)

I Thessalonians 5:23

Created by Andrea L. Russell

www.ingramcontent.com/pod-product-compliance
Lightning Source LLC
Chambersburg PA
CBHW051839090426
42736CB00011B/1887